IN DEPTH
URBAN DOMESTICITIES TODAY

T0400541

Thank you, Amador Rodríguez Ramírez, Brian Janusiak, Elizabeth Beer, Iasson Tsakonas, Janaina Tschäpe, Monica Healy, Oke Hauser, Sam Alison-Mayne, Sebastian Mendez, Robert Doser, and Howard Katz, for your trust.

Thank you, Catherine Ingraham, Emanuele Coccia, Il Kim, Justin Davidson, and Mohamed Sharif, for your encouragement.

Thank you, Andrew Reyniak, Geoff Han, Ilias Papageorgiou, and Ted Kane, for your collaboration.

Thank you, Elise Jaffe + Jeffrey Brown, for your generosity, and much appreciation for initial impulse given by the Cornell AAP's Professional Development Fund.

Finally, thank you, Summer Liu, for your dedication.

Editors: Jing Liu, Florian Idenburg
Photography: Iwan Baan, Naho Kubota
Copy Editing Keonaona Peterson
Proofreading: Ian McDonald
Publishing Coordination: Hester van den Bold
Production (SO-IL): Jing Liu, Florian Idenburg, Summer Liu, Kevin Lamyuktseung, Ted Baab, Michael Levy, Xingyao Wang, Cynthia Zhang, Demetri Lampris
Graphic design: Geoff Han
Lithography: Sebastiaan Hanekroot, Colour & Books
Production: Jos Morree, Fine Books
Printing: Wilco Art Books

Lars Müller Publishers
Zurich, Switzerland
www.lars-mueller-publishers.com

ISBN 978-3-03778-757-1

Distributed in North America, Latin America and the Caribbean by ARTBOOK | D.A.P.

www.artbook.com

Printed in the Netherlands

LIFE
IWAN BAAN, ELIZABETH BEER, FLORIAN IDENBURG, BRIAN JANUSIAK, DEAN KAUFMAN & NAHO KUBOTA

A porous ground level at Las Américas filters urbanity, accommodating the wheels that roll through

In a remote alley, a breathable sculpture appears, cocooning a nomadic urban space for living

The sun animates Las Américas' deep facade as the
day progresses

Personalized interior of Las Américas

A "Telematic House" (a term coined by Milanese designer Ugo La Pietra in 1983 referring to digital technologies' presence in domestic space) in Las Américas

Arriving home at Clifton

Shades and layers at Bergen

Breathe's skin filters the air

Dog living in Bergen

Dog living in 450 Warren

Dog and his best friend living in Las Américas

Shaping up at Warren 450

Drawing against the garden on Adelphi

Making art at Clifton

Breathe, while accommodating domesticity, also animates its surroundings

Pregame at Las Américas

Moving into Las Américas

Plants outside Clifton

Plants in Clifton

Halloween at Warren

Lunch time in a nook at Bergen

Night time on a balcony at Bergen

Relaxing in Las Américas

Gathering at Adelphi

Breakfast at Adelphi

A bed at Breathe

A bed at Las Américas

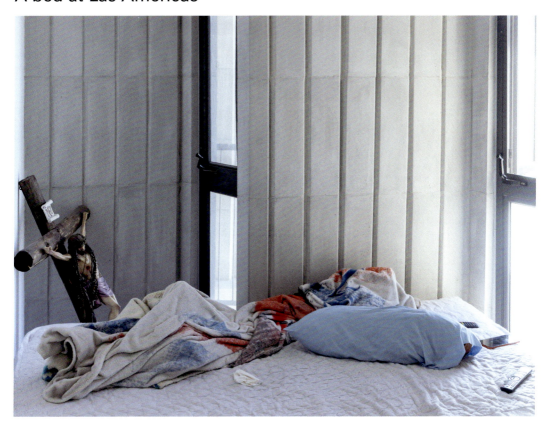

Cat living in Las Américas

Cat and her best friend living in Las Américas

INTRODUCTION
JING LIU

Home is where one starts from. As we grow older
The world becomes stranger, the pattern more
    complicated
Of dead and living. Not the intense moment
Isolated, with no before and after,
But a lifetime burning in every moment
And not the lifetime of one man only
But of old stones that cannot be deciphered.
There is a time for the evening under starlight,
A time for the evening under lamplight
(The evening with the photograph album).
......
In my end is my beginning.
  – T. S. Eliot, *Four Quartets*, Part II: "East Coker" (1943)

Home – an innermost sanctum, a well of longing or a simple patch where our bodies can lie down – is where we all start from.

When I close my eyes and imagine the place called *home*, I see dappled light rubbing on the wooden windowsill whose edges are no longer sharp but rounded and smooth, thickened by layers upon layers of paint; the light slips and glides until it gently falls on the tiled floor, whose cracks and wrinkles are its charm. Afloat in the air are the dampened laughter of women next door, bicycle bells ringing outside, sparrows on the electrical lines, and a sweet hint of sesame oil and rice vinegar.

All of a sudden, development steamrolled my sleepy hometown. Its feathery charms stood little chance against the mighty neoliberal engine. Overnight, thousands of old oak and plane trees were cut down to make oversized asphalt streets all over the city, which were then decorated with the confetti of KFCs and McDonald's. Wooden houses and stone courtyards were replaced with marching orders of concrete housing blocks, which, in turn, were quickly torn down to make way for shiny high-rises. Crusts and dust drowned the streets and pushed an entire generation of youth indoors.

When we sat down to compile our recent projects for the home into a book, it was clear that this was not about housing. We won't attempt to theorize housing, propose sweeping solutions to its problems, or present the projects as a set of metaphysical ideals. Instead, this book and the projects included in and beyond these pages are our attempts to enchant the house; as rogue architects who stretch codes, inhabit depths, and turn "old stones"; to find a home for things not for sale and which don't belong to anyone; to question if *housing for all* (instead of, for example, *a home for everyone*) should be the yardstick for the shelters of our humanity; to experiment; and to follow other logics, like Alice in Wonderland.[1]

Modernity, which drowned my childhood home, had two vectors. In its rearview, old customs and stifling structures were flushed out, industry was to be integrated with the everyday and the emergence of a new consciousness of the common man was promised. In its abyss ahead, however, the instruments that wrought the modern world – mass production and economic life – bent the vector by extracting enormous energy and resources and directing them toward the collective so that *home* – the site of nonconforming idiosyncrasies, unresolved mysteries, intangible ancestral ties, unsanctioned futurities, and infinite shapes of togetherness – was emptied and made ancillary to the city. Hannes Meyer, the Bauhaus director at the height of

1   *Alice's Adventures in Wonderland* (1865) is an English children's novel by Lewis Carroll, a mathematician at Oxford University. Ending the era of didacticism in children's literature, the book delighted children and adults with nonsensical and paradoxical tales, in a world bounded by rules not of our world. Unlike the creatures of Wonderland, who approach their world's wonders uncritically, Alice continues to look for rules as the story progresses, mirroring Carroll's own search for logic in the emergent non-Euclidean geometry then in development at the time.

the industrializing Weimar Republic, declared unequivocally: "The surest sign of true community is the satisfaction of the same needs by the same means,"[2] accompanied by a radical portrayal of the new domesticity, the *Co-op Interieur* (Fig. 1).[3]

> The upshot of such a collective demand is the standard product. […] They are apparatus in the mechanization of our daily life. They are manufactured in quantity as a mass-produced device, as a mass-produced structural element, as a mass-produced house. […] The degree of our standardization is an index of our communal productive system.[4]

Critics throughout the modern ages – Henrik Ibsen, Walter Benjamin, and Martin Heidegger alike – have all reflected on the blight of the *interieur*, often to a melancholic or nihilistic end.[5] The irony is that as distasteful as Meyer's words might

2   Hannes Meyer, "Die Neue Welt," *Das Werk* 13, no. 7 (1926). Hannes Meyer was the second director of the Bauhaus. During his short tenure (1928–30), Meyer aimed to transform architectural production into a means for the working class to fight against capitalism. He believed that an egalitarian society mass-produced its own architecture and that the role of an architect was to organize the interplay between technology (machine) and the collective body (the people). This transformed the esoteric roles architects played historically to one that was no different from other workers. Meyer downplayed the role of the individual and communities, and elevated that of the machine and collective in the production of society. Meyer traveled to the USSR after the Bauhaus, and was an editor of *Die Neue Welt* – a communist newspaper issued from Alsace, France, between 1933 and 1934, before moving permanently to Mexico in 1938.

3   Captioned "Die Wohnung" (The Apartment), the illustration accompanied Meyer's article. It depicted a sparse room, staged with a headboardless bed, a round table just big enough for the gramophone placed on top of it, and a folded chair hung on the wall. It was a cropped version in which another folding chair and a wall shelf with bottles of powder were ostensibly left out, possibly because of their suggestion of social interaction and accumulation of goods in private space.

4   Meyer, "Die Neue Welt."

5   Henrik Ibsen in *The Master Builder* (1892), Walter Benjamin in

Fig. 1: *Co-op Interieur*, composed by Hannes Meyer, 1926.

sound to the free people of modernity, most people today live in some version of the *Co-op Interieur* – their spatial uniformity characterized by tightly packed rectangular rooms linked by highly efficient corridors and hermetically sealed to minimize exchanges with all kinds of "others." Both the philosophical gaze and our empirical knowledge seem to declare the architecture of the *interieur* of the commoners doomed. On this topic, Hannah Arendt illuminates a crucial element at risk in the discourse – care and tenderness:

> The French have become masters in the art of being happy among 'small things,' within the space of their own four walls, between chest and bed, table and chair, dog and cat and flowerpot, extending to these things a care and tenderness which, in a world where rapid industrialization constantly kills off the things of yesterday to produce today's objects, may even appear to be the world's last, purely humane corner.[6]

Care and tenderness are not exclusive to the French, nor do they have to be limited to the "small things" within four walls. In fact, there existed many types of domestic architecture that housed not only our bodies and their material extensions but also care and tenderness toward other people, lives, and things. *Siheyuan* (Fig. 2) (Chinese courtyard houses) and *rumah adat* (Fig. 3) (elaborately evolved longhouses in Indonesia) alike, where generations after generations gathered in harmony as well as in distress, have woven a rich web of rituals, customs, and social relations around the care for our kin under one roof. However, modernity saw them as unsanitary and archaic, treated them as a nuisance and obstacle to urbanization, and demolished them en masse. The Japanese *machiya*, the French

One-Way Street (1928), and Martin Heideger in *Building Dwelling Thinking* (1971) are a few among many philosophers who contemplated the problem of dwelling.

6   Hannah Arendt, *The Human Condition* (Chicago: University of Chicago Press, 1958), 52.

Fig. 2: View of traditional *Siheyuan* courtyard.

Fig. 3: Traditional *rumah adat* in south Nias, Indonesia.

Fig. 4: Dutch street scene by a canal, Willem Koekkoek (1839–1895).

maison, or the English *mansion* socialized craft, commerce, family traditions, and quotidian life together as interdependent blocks. They have now largely been relegated to business establishments. The Italian *villa*, where one room flows into another and the world outside flows through the domestic spaces inside in a way that individual parts cannot be secreted from the whole of life, are now sites of museums and hospitality, occasioning the extraordinary rather than the ordinary. The myriad nomadic structures such as *pao*, *teepee*, and *igloo*, enablers of humans' embedded existence in nature, are popularized as glamping sites during tourist seasons in heavily managed and readily consumable "natures." The tally goes on.

How did *house* become the sole survivor in the kaleidoscopic world of domestic architecture?

Etymologically, *house* traces its origin back to the Germanic *haus*, which refers to livestock and grain-storage structures. People did not live in the *haus*. In the seventeenth century, Dutch merchants moved into the *huis* and made a palace for the bourgeoisie out of it. Cranes installed on gables hoisted goods up and down the slender canal houses – a compressed hybrid between the Germanic *haus* and Venetian *palazzo*, the ground level visible to passersby to promote business while residents climbed steep, narrow stairways and navigated corridors among their accumulated possessions (Fig. 4). One could argue that the Dutch merchants of the Golden Age fused two otherwise unrelated concepts – one of the safe-keeping of material assets and the other of the expression of subjective personhood – in the *huis* through ad hoc experimentation.

Today's housing practice – designing urban domesticity for an ever-increasing population and goods – is anything but ad hoc. It is tightly governed by the holy trinity of efficiency, density, and economy with very little room for experimentation. Once a rich site of crafts, where care and tenderness were extended to animate the material world around us, homes are now impoverished with standardized industrial materials quickly put together, requiring minimal maintenance, and anticipating a short shelf life. Amid rising land costs, the spaces not included in the NFA (Net Floor Area) and therefore not for sale (i.e. code-required exterior for legal light and air, cores for distribution of resources, courts for common leisure, and corridors for circulation) are ever-shrinking because they are unsellable. But no matter how reduced the spatial experience of urban domesticity has become, the doctrine of perpetual shortage renders any departure from the most efficient and cost-effective practices immoral.

Up against the tyranny of efficiency, one old stone we attempted to turn is that of the double-loaded corridor.[7] In "Cancel the Corridor" (p. 98), Nicolas Kemper traces the origin of the corridor back to fourteenth-century German barrack design as the passage for runners carrying the orders of commanders. Housing doubled down on this military disposition, loading it with apartments on both sides; slicing the *interieurs* in half; taking away half of their light and air; and dumping our bodies in long, dreary collectors of anonymous doors with low ceilings, cheap carpets, no daylight, and no escape. We have looked for alternatives in the Japanese *engawa*[8] (Fig. 5) or the *streets in*

7   The double-loaded corridor is an arrangement of residential units on both sides of a long hallway, usually with two exit stairs near the opposite ends.

8   *Engawa* refers to the outer perimeter under a roof overhang in traditional Japanese architecture. The original immigrants to Japan (Yayoi) arrived from the south and brought Shinto, a theology that believes spirits live in the natural world, and its architecture to the islands, characterized by thatch roofs, unfinished wooden pillars, and floors suspended above the ground.

To protect against strong winds, heavy rains, and occasional earthquakes, these structures were usually built with several rows of posts, with the living quarters enclosed by partitions fixed to the inner posts. The area between the inner and outer posts close to the edge of the roof became a covered exterior space, a predecessor of *engawa*.
   During the Heian period (794-1185 AD), aristocrats started to construct palaces influenced by China's Tang culture, and the original tropical pavilions were conglomerated into larger complexes with *engawa* providing a continuous circulation

the air (Fig. 6), both allowing us to take a step outside and make a small piece of the *exterieur* our own.[9] In *Pillow Book*, court lady Sei Shonagon recorded with much enthusiasm the "pleasant things" – intangible delights in and around the Heian palace where she lived:

> In winter, the early mornings. It is beautiful indeed when the snow has fallen during the night, but splendid too when the ground is white with frost; or even when there is no snow or frost, but it is simply very cold and the attendants hurry from room to room stirring up the fires and bringing charcoal.[10]

surrounding the inner spaces, maintaining overall openness and fluidity. As Zen Buddhism (a new religion from Tang culture) sought to transcend the merely utilitarian and attend as closely to humans' interior needs as to their physical comfort, Japanese architecture after the Heian period retained a simplicity and connection to nature. There was minimal or no furniture in any rooms, so residents sat, ate, and slept on the floor. They took off their shoes in the *engawa* to maintain cleanliness. *Engawa* also made stepping out into the gardens easy from any room. Over the centuries, *engawa* became the most evocative multiple relational and liminal space that defines Japanese architecture.

9   In 1919, the Spangen Quarter, designed by Michiel Brinkman, opened in Rotterdam with a four-story, one-kilometer-long perimeter block introducing a new density to the modernizing city. On the interior of the block, a continuous exterior corridor – a "street in the air" – lined the third floor of the housing block, visually, experientially, and functionally connecting the upper levels to a new ground. Streets in the air appeared in many successful large-scale housing proposals throughout the twentieth century, often in temperate climates, from Le Corbusier's Unité d'Habitation in Marseille to Luigi Carlo Daneri's INA-Casa in Genoa, to Ricardo Bofill's Walden 7 in Barcelona and SANAA's Kitagata in Gifu. However, its association with troubled projects such as Pruitt-Igoe in St. Louis and Robin Hood Gardens in London tarnished its reputation as a socialized circulatory element.

10   Sei Shonagon, *The Pillow Book*, ed. and trans. Ivan Morris (New York: Penguin Books, 1971), 21. *The Pillow Book*, a volume of musings by court lady Sei Shonagon during the late Heian period, is a valuable historical document revealing the details of life and aesthetics of the imperial court of her time. While Shonagon never meant her writing for any audience but her own enjoyment, her keen observations, lively descriptions, and poetic prose make the book a literary classic.

Fig. 5: *Kunai-kyo (or Sei Shonagon?), from an untitled series of classical beauties*, Torii Kiyonaga, ca. 1784.

Fig. 6: Golden Lane: Street Deck. Alison and Peter Smithson, 1952.

The attendants hurried in the *engawa*, the enchanted space between the extended floor and the roof overhang that gently mediated between the warm *interieur* and frosty *exterieur*.

In impoverished postwar London, Alison and Peter Smithson's joyful collages depicting a spontaneous sociality in the "streets in the air" articulated a sorely needed utopian vision. In their Golden Lane competition entry, "the daily grind of working-class life is miraculously swapped for glamor, youth, and health," featuring a man on all fours playing with a toddler, Marilyn Monroe, and the baseball player Joe DiMaggio. Many of these council estates succumbed to chronic neglect and were cleared away for new developments in recent decades, but documentarians and journalists were able to capture with their cameras the streets in the air teeming with human life and human love until their final days.[11] In the Hyde Park flats in Sheffield, demolished barely twenty years after its construction, paper girls roller-skated down the halls (Fig. 7), a milkman delivered dairy products in steel wagons, cousins exchanged a moment of friendly mockery, and women gossiped about social sundries at the doorways. Even with tough times befalling them and many residents unemployed after the closure of the pits and the steelworks, they were still fond of their homes on these "streets" and didn't want to move.

Our first project with Tankhouse[12] – 450 Warren Street (p. 220), completed in 2021, did away with double-loaded corridors and

11   Bill Stephenson, "Streets in the Sky: Portraits of the Last Tenants at Hyde Park Flats, Sheffield 1988," https://billstephenson.co.uk/streets-in-the-sky-hyde-park-flats-1988/; accessed June 6, 2024.

12   Tankhouse is a development company in Brooklyn founded in 2013 by Sam Alison Mayne and Sebastian Mendez. Sam and Sebastian met working on the Sperone Westwater Art Gallery in New York City, designed by Foster+Partners. Sebastian was the project architect and Sam was the construction manager working for Sciame (a renowned construction company based in New York City). When the two architecture lovers established Tankhouse to develop multifamily residential properties, they also met SO–IL. Together

Fig. 7: Roller-skating paper-delivery girls Anita Cutts and Emma Guirham.

the 80% efficiency ratio – two golden rules of the New York City housing design and development matrix. The project scrupulously transformed one of its two meanings of egress into a set of covered exterior stairs and corridors, encircling a common courtyard outside the minimum legal light-and-air requirement. Its voluminous and porous body doubled the Net Floor Area and maximized the buildable envelope, so it was possible to make the *exterieur* livable.[13] It was a continuation of early experiments like Party Wall (p. 198) and tiNY (p. 230), where the idea of utilizing single-loaded corridors as egress – maximizing light, view, and cross ventilation – was developed and promised to bring back the "pleasant things" of a winter morning; and a more finely attuned version of Las Américas (p. 238), where the combination of exterior corridors and courtyards reshaped the architectural body and promised to bring back the dampened laughter of neighbors, the milkman, and roller-skaters (Fig. 8).

If *engawa* makes a patch of the *exterieur* our own, and the *street in the air* socializes our daily encounters, then *court* mediates our relationship with the unknown and unowned by interiorizing, without defining, the *exterieur*. It was the earliest architectural form of human communion, dating as far back as the Neolithic age, when people deposited remains of their ancestors, animal kin, and broken pottery in circular megaliths (Fig. 9). Travelers arrived from all directions, took passages framed by the stones, and were brought together by spirits

we have worked to aerate the housing paradigm.

13 At 450 Warren, protected curtilages are fitted with benches and at-grade bike parking, linked by the playfully sculpted exterior egress, eliminating dreadful double-loaded corridors and activating the space between the *interieur* and the *exterieur*. Generously planted courtyards and side yards, protected balconies, and terraces make living outside possible without needing air conditioning, layers upon layers of finishes, and expensive equipment. Cool summer breeze breathes through the shaded courtyard, bringing cross ventilation to every unit; winter blizzards are shielded by the solid corners, while warm afternoon sun slips in from the sides. Although these livable exterior spaces are not sellable and don't belong to anyone, they define a generous way of living with one another for the residents.

Fig. 8: Roller-skaters in Las Américas, a high-density, social-housing prototype in León, Mexico.

Fig. 9: Beltany stone circle.

outside the self and beyond here and now. In early settlements and throughout history, courtyard houses were the most common typology for domestic architecture around the world, creating shelters for bonded kin and nurturing their shared futurity. *Court* is the antithesis of an attic or basement where the past is kept in captivity for private visitation or otherwise left forgotten to collect dust. It holds the past and the coming in a shared present. Metaphysically, *court* creates a finiteness in nature and a horizon close to *home*. The Renaissance pried open these sacred courts, and the Enlightenment set out to conquer the infinite. With the last pockets of *court* driven out by liberal urbanization, we might lose this physical and spatial form of a shared, enduring unknown entirely.

In "Codes of Living" (p. 82), Ted Baab traces the history of the formulation and legal enforcement of *court* in New York City dating from the anti-tenement New Law of 1901 (predecessor of the first complete Zoning Resolution in 1916), in response to photojournalist Jacob Riis's documentation of "the dark and grim slum conditions of the Lower Manhattan tenements." (Fig. 10). From this initial singular and somewhat paternalistic vision, the plethora of desires of individuals, companies, or city governments to shape the city's fabric to their own interests over time has made the Zoning Resolution a "hyper-dimensional reality." These pockets of porosity have become a labyrinth most architects do not dare to venture into. However, if we are willing to leave old logic behind, there is a wonderous world to explore among the diminishing courts in our cities today and in the labyrinth of manifold ideas. Following the success of 450 Warren, we continue to develop projects with Tankhouse in which the court acts as the primary agent in determining unit assembly, away from the tyranny of double-loaded corridors and efficiency ratio. At 144 Vanderbilt (p. 248) and 450 Union (p. 256), the collection of backyards, side yards, and setbacks are complemented by additional rooftop terraces, shifting structural grids, and drawing intentional relationships with neighboring buildings, so that

Fig. 10: Early New York tenement conditions, ca. 1900.

together they create a series of courts on multiple levels and in multiple directions.

As human habitation continues to weigh down the planet, putting our collective *home* – Earth – at risk, density is a necessary planning instrument for other species to survive alongside us. However, the logic of density projected in architectural forms like the Hong Kong towers and MIH (Mandatory Inclusionary Housing) developments in New York City hardly produces anything social or human. In Las Américas (p. 238), a housing prototype initiated by the city of León, MX, to reverse the sprawl of migrant settlements (Fig. 11), it was as important to create a nurturing home for the residents and a proud icon for the neighborhood as it was to make high-density housing in the city. In 450 Union (p. 256), an upzone development that needs to meet the MIH requirements and a tight budget, the principles developed in the courts and corridors from earlier projects still managed to produce airy and sundry social porosity in the vertical village. Ultimately, *home* is relational, not teleological, and *housing* is not merely the act of putting objects and bodies in storage. We need to pay extra attention to the relationships engendered inside these dense urban domesticities as they will replace the great "nature" as the predominant environment that shapes our humanity.

Besides zoning codes and building codes, energy codes are another hyperdimensional example of a collection of past desires and current compromises, with many old stones to be turned. Karilyn Johanesen's text on the envelope (p. 107) traces how the economic, regulatory, and physical thresholds that used to rift in and out of each other and are permeated by a rich world of social habitation, zones of microclimates, and spatial types have collapsed into a single line of the envelope today. This creates a sharp division between inside and outside, denotes a two-dimensional representational image, and is increasingly hardened by the environmental-performance matrix.

Fig. 11: Urban sprawl in Mexico.

The problem of the envelope stems from the *core*. In his critique "A Home Is Not a House," Reyner Banham predicted,

> with very little exaggeration, this baroque ensemble of domestic gadgetry epitomizes the intestinal complexity of gracious living. [...] If mechanical services continue to accumulate at this rate it may be possible to omit the house in fact.[14]

The baroque "gadgetry" core in our modern houses are, akin to Deleuze and Guattari's "desiring-machines," mechanisms to extract, appropriate, and incorporate energy and resources outside oneself into oneself. They are disguised vestiges of the premodern world: the dichotomy between the served and the serving. Basement servants' quarters, hidden stairways, and corridors turned into machines in undercrofts and pipes and ducts in chases. As mass production banished the serving further away, out of sight, with infrastructural tentacles delivering energy and resources optically free from histories and consequences, our hidden debts mounted exponentially. Current energy codes – conservative in nature, stipulated by passive strategies, and reliant on a high-performing envelope (more embodied energy) – are merely a medical approach to our diagnosis without questioning the moral basis of this unidirectional dependency.

If freedom is an essential tenet of modernity, then we should strive to be free from the serving and debts and establish a symbiotic relationship with the "others." The architectural core needs to flow both ways – serving and being served by our collective big home. To do so, we need to consider the archi-

14 Reyer Banham, "A Home Is Not a House," *Art in America* 2 (April 1965). In this article, architectural critic Banham attacks North American houses, built without proper protection from cold and warm weather, based upon a widespread use of heating pumps, a general waste of energy, and the production of an "environmental machinery."

tectural shell not only as a conservator and weather barrier but also as an atmosphere remediator, energy creator, and water harvester, and consider the entire house a site of localized metabolic processes that are energy- and resource-positive. In the experimental project, Breathe (p. 170), a mini house for three, as it inserts itself in a dead-end alley in Milan, also takes in rainwater, daylight, and views; it needs little furniture, collects pollutants from the atmosphere, and lights up warmly at night like a lantern. Breathe is a new "primitive hut" (Fig. 12).[15] It seeks to defy the consumptive habits of modern life, land lightly on the ground, take what's abundant around it, and offer what's scarce back. The self-sufficient PetalHouse (p. 206), a prefabricated ADU designed for the city of Los Angeles, embraces smallness, adds density, and a new income stream in the backyard without requiring heavy logistics and onerous site work.[16] It moves in like a petal. Much work must be done to free our houses from the "baroque core," extend care and

15 "Primitive Hut" explores the anthropological relationship between human and the natural environments as the fundamental basis for the creation of architecture, theorized in particular by Abbé Marc-Antoine Laugier in *An Essay on Architecture* published in 1753 – in the Age of Enlightenment. Architecture in France during this period was defined predominantly by the Baroque style with its excessive ornamentation and religious iconography. Rather than being concerned with the search for meaning and the overanalysis of the representational elements of architecture, Laugier's essay proposed that the idea of noble and formal architecture was found not in its ornamentation but in its true underlying fundamentals. To Laugier, the primitive hut was the highest virtue that architecture should aspire to.

16 According to the definition from the American Planning Association, an accessory dwelling unit (ADU) is a small, independent residential dwelling unit located on the same lot as a stand-alone (i.e. detached) single-family home. ADUs have the potential to increase housing affordability (both for homeowners and tenants), create a wider range of housing options within the community, enable seniors to stay near family as they age, and facilitate better use of the existing housing fabric in established neighborhoods. In recent years, many cities and counties have signaled support for ADUs in their plans and adopted zoning regulations that permit ADUs in low-density residential areas.

Fig. 12: Allegorical engraving of the Vitruvian Primitive Hut. Frontispiece of Marc-Antoine Laugier, *Essai sur l'architecture*, 2nd ed. 1755, by Charles Eisen (1720–1778).

Fig. 13: *Il Commutatore*, Ugo La Pietra (from the Disequilibrating System research), 1970.

tenderness toward our collective big home, and learn how to be a chameleon and octopus rather than a hard-shelled turtle. Chameleons and octopi possess extraordinary intelligence in their ability to read the environment, adapt and hack it, become part of it rather than be in opposition – and all with a sense of humor and humility. With humor, Milanese designer Ugo La Pietra hacked the regime of urbanization and its mechanistic operations with his whimsical ad hoc "living" objects, domesticating the usually impersonal, sanitized city into his home (Fig. 13).[17] When Lithuanian-born American artist Aleksandra Kasuba transformed her townhouse in Manhattan, she complicated the generic box with stretched fabrics and sensorial experiences through materially rich, tactile surfaces and imbuing the rectilinear plan with a delicate tension (Fig. 14).[18] *Transversality* – a term coined by Japanese architect Kazuo Shinohara, whose domestic projects are concerned with the intersectionality of Japanese values and Western technologies

17 From the 1960s onwards, Italian designer Ugo La Pietra's militant, anti-design project "Abitare e Essere Ovunque a Casa Propria" (To Live Is to Be Everywhere in Your Own Home) illustrated the possibility of appropriating the public realm as domestic space through a collection of makeshift furniture and spontaneous occupations. La Pietra shaved himself in storefront mirrors; transformed an abandoned, plastic street barrier into a sofa; and slept in the middle of the street using a portable "easel" bed. In these ad hoc situations, *home* is no longer limited within four walls; rather, it can be constructed as a dynamic domestic practice set up between the city and the individual. In resuscitating this relationship and insisting on exchange and negotiation between the two entities, isolated individuals can once again become aware of their intrinsic desire to connect with others and experiment with how such a connection can be established. La Pietra's do-it-yourself, handcrafted objects, documenting and framing of the city through the lens of domesticity, and instructions for a playful spatial practice challenged the notion that architecture is limited to static and singular entities, expanding it to include the temporal and the ritualistic.

18 Aleksandra Kasuba, a Lithuanian-American artist, built the *Live-in-Environment* inside her brownstone apartment in New York City between 1971 and 1972, intending to "abolish the 90-degree angle and introduce a variety of spatial experiences without imitating nature." Translucent, elastic nylon, a fabric used primarily for military parachutes,

Fig. 14: *The Live-in Environment*, Aleksandra Kasuba, 1971–72.

Figs. 15–17: *Pao I*, 1985. "Pao: Dwellings for the Tokyo Nomad Woman" by Toyo Ito.

Fig. 18: *Pao II*, 1989. "Pao: Dwellings For the Tokyo Nomad Woman" by Toyo Ito.

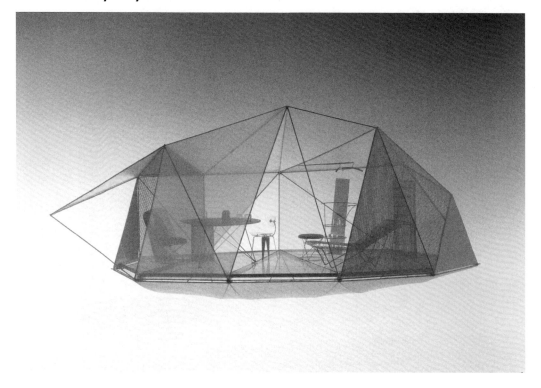

– embraces the vitality arising from cutting across, chaos, turbulence, and confrontation as "the world flow[s] ceaselessly through the small spaces" within the walls of the *house*.[19] When we transformed artist Janaina Tschape's home and studio (p. 182) and designers Elizabeth Beer and Brian Janusiak's family home (p. 176), we let sunlight and starlight pour in from above, connecting the *interieur* to the circadian and cosmic. Stairs and exposed structures are intentionally placed on opposite sides of the house, claiming their rightful space and motivating the functional elements to produce transversality. The exchange between inside and outside is no longer limited to planar facade fenestrations but variegated and layered through narrow slits, layered balconies, and protruding terraces. *House* need not be passive or neutral but the site for highly personal engagement with others and beyond.

The reconceptualization of *house* from passive to active, from collective to personal, from generic to specific, from singular to multiple, and from consumptive to care is not only moral but also existential. In 1985, a young Kazuyo Sejima enacted the "Tokyo Nomad Woman" in Toyo Ito's *Pao I* – a harbinger of our own obsolescence in the coming world (Figs. 15–17).[20] Sitting

was stretched between the ceiling and the floor in fluid lines, resulting in sensuous curves and soft tensions. The artist redrew the generic, rectangular plan of the brownstone with sculpted daylight, layers of translucency, and infinite depth of space. Instead of using typical furniture to assign functions to spaces, Kasuba deployed crochet, mohair, mirror, sound, and scent to articulate the variety of experiences in each room.

19 Shinohara Kazuo, "Beyond Symbol Spaces: An Introduction to Primary Spaces as Functional Spaces," *The Japan Architect* (April 1971): 81–88.

20 *Pao* is the name for the Mongolian tent for nomadic people whose livelihood depends on the natural environment. In Toyo Ito's *Pao I* the Tokyo Nomad Woman's material possessions are minimal but of symbolic significance – a clothing rack, a makeup stand, and a mirror. By performing the daily ritual of putting on makeup in front of the mirror, she sees her own image in the context that surrounds her.

Fig. 19: *The Environment-Bubble*, François Dallegret, from Reyner Banham, "A Home Is Not a House," *Art in America* (April 1965).

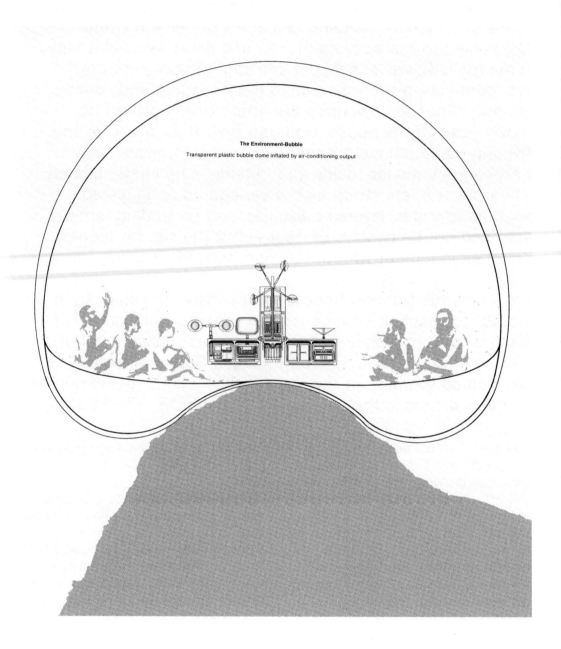

between a clothing rack, mirror, and makeup table inside a transparent structure, Tokyo Nomad Woman's image as a consumer rather than a producer or caretaker signaled empowerment and freedom. But as she remains afloat in the hypermediatized urban environment like the seeds of a dandelion, she can also be dissolved without a trace. Banham's and Dallegret's *Environment-Bubble* (Fig. 19) and Tokyo Nomad Woman's "Pao" render the subjects vulnerable.[21] In houses where praxis is shortchanged by performance, we become subsumed into large systems, our bodies are militarized and social sundries annihilated, and diminishing porosity mirrors the disappearance of our shared unknown; humanity is besieged. Such a crisis is underscored by contemporary thinkers like Emanuele Coccia, who says that it will be WhatsApp rather than Le Corbusier's Modulor that's the model for communal housing.[22]

Almost a hundred years ago, Virginia Woolf wrote about a room of one's own, where one can "draw the curtains; to shut out distractions; to light the lamp; to narrow the inquiry and to ask the historian." Without it, "the great problem of the true nature of women and the true nature of fiction [is] unsolved."[23] If we asked the historian today about the fate of our *home*, what might she tell us? She might say that while a *house* can

21 The *Environment-Bubble* is a transparent, plastic bubble dome inflated by air-conditioning output. It appears in an illustration by François Dallegret, accompanying Reyner Banham's text "A Home Is Not a House."

22 Emanuele Coccia, *Filosofia della Casa: Lo Spazio Domestico e la Felicità* (*Philosophy of the Home. The Domestic Space and Happiness*) (Turin: Einaudi, 2021), 113.

23 In 1928, in front of an audience at Newnham College, Cambridge University, Virginia Woolf delivered the following words: "All I could do was offer you an opinion upon one minor point – a woman must have money and a room of her own if she is to write fiction; and that, as you will see, leaves the great problem of the true nature of woman and the true nature of fiction unsolved." These lectures formed the basis of the book she published the following year, *A Room of One's Own*. As Woolf promised, the seminal text set the scene for the study of women's writing and that of women's history.

be produced, a *home* can only emerge from praxis; that the art of designing the most ordinary sites of our quotidian life urgently needs abundant experimentation; that it is necessary to adapt and adjust its architectural and physical languages while holding the spatial, material, economic, and ecological systems in a precarious tension; that we need to rediscover and learn to live in liminal spaces – in-depth; that among fragments of past dreams and heaps of current compromises, there is a new unknown that we can tenderly hold together; and that insofar as our *homes* inhabit our collective big *home*, their bodies incorporate other constantly evolving bodies, and their codes encode that of our togetherness and, always revising, they promise to bring about the vital materialization of the divine desires of life.

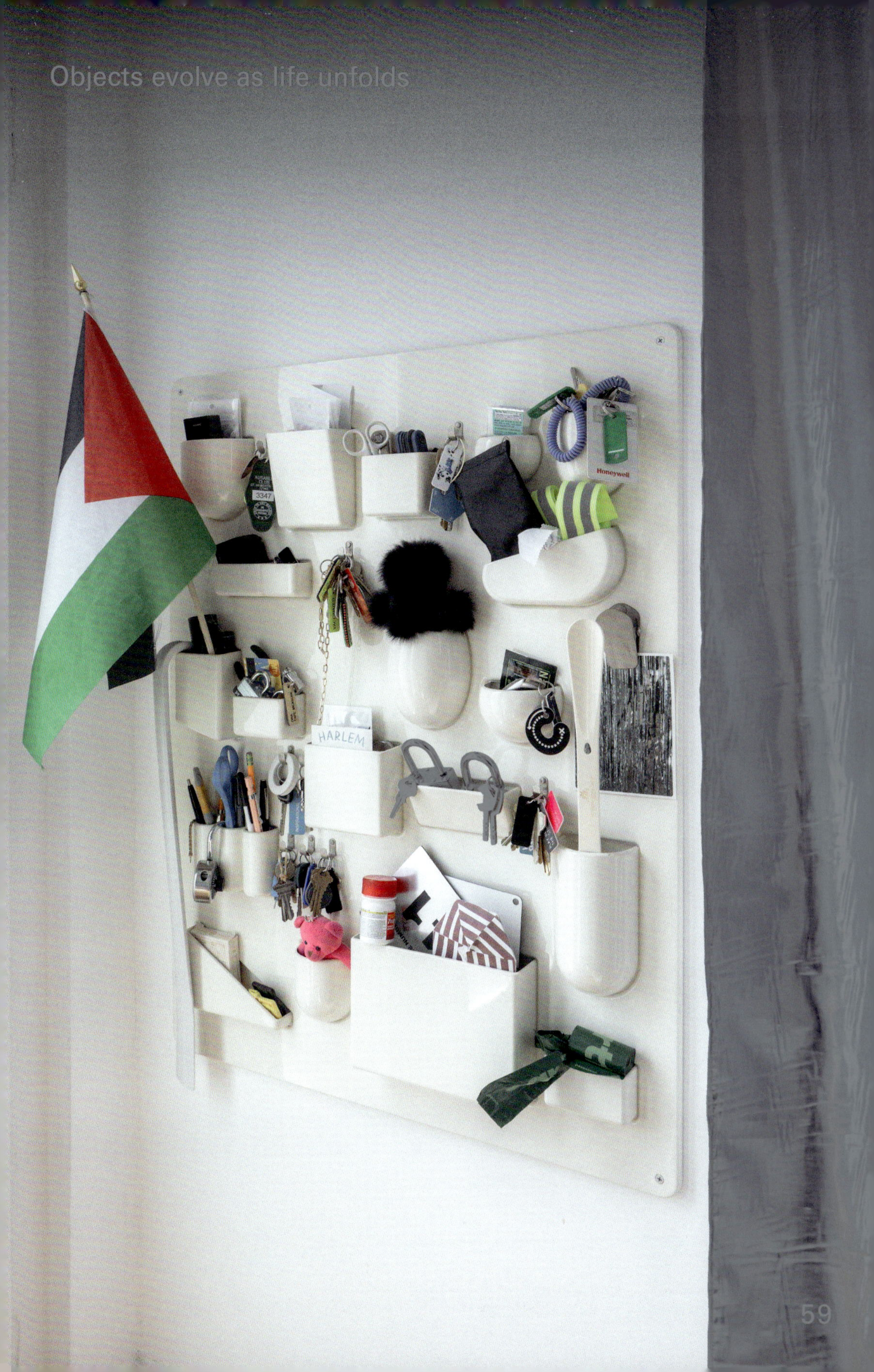
3347
HARLEM
Honeywell

On the parlor level of Bergen, a curved pantry wall creates a soft line between living and kitchen areas

Lines and circles at multiple scales accentuate the
luminous interior

Subtle colors tint the various sources of light

A second spiral stair burrowing into the garden apartment and cellar is lined with carpet to dampen sound, creating a moment of secrecy and intimacy

Green metal, chrome wire, and brown leather

68

The garden apartment opens to a generous covered patio

Every level opens out to a porous balcony

73

The distinctive facade is a tapestry of varying brick patterns

ESSAYS

CODES OF LIVING
TED BAAB

Delirious New York, Rem Koolhaas's 1978 manifesto, proposed that the city's true innovation is its mess; the city as a machine for serendipity, layering many coincident cities on top of one another. The city needs us to bump up against one another, to catch glimpses of parallel realities outside our own, offering new paths and new lives. This vision of hyperdimensional reality makes the prospect of building regulations reconciling private ambitions with public responsibility a seemingly impossible task.

***

Jacob Riis's famed 1890 book, *How the Other Half Lives*, made newly visible the grim slum conditions of the Lower Manhattan tenements that housed many of the city's new Irish and Italian immigrants (Fig. 1). His photos bore witness to stagnant and windowless mazes of rooms struggling to house the city's tired laboring class. Hastily built structures hardly kept out weather and vermin, and were so close together that fear of disease and fire were omnipresent.

Before the first building and zoning codes, buildings in the city had a life of their own.[1] City blocks were filled lot line to lot line (Fig. 2). Landlords decided what dimensions and facilities constituted sufficient conditions for living. Some had running water; others had windows in just a few of their rooms; many had neither (Fig. 3). Without a framework holding everyone to account, there was no way to set standards for building, let alone conditions for living.

1   The first building-construction code was created in 1899, according to the preface of the 2022 building code.

Fig. 1: Riis captured tenement life in photographs, 1890–94. Most living quarters did not have windows or any access to exterior light or air.

Fig. 2: An 1894 map shows a section of Lower Manhattan with population density exceeding 900 persons per acre.

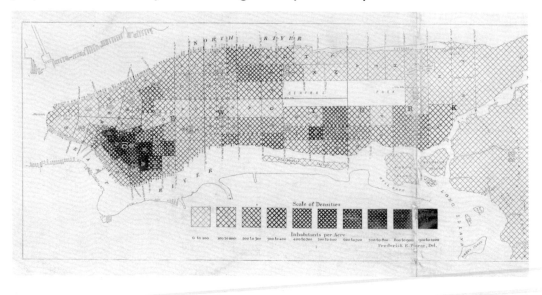

Fig. 3: A full block of tenement housing, no windows in sight.

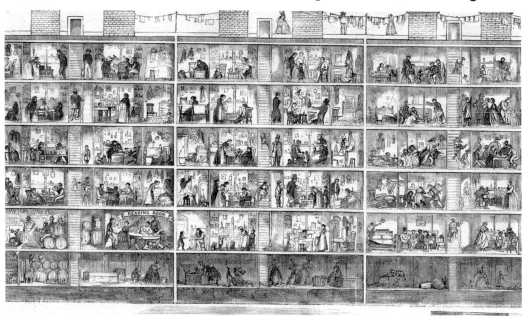

The anti-tenement New Law of 1901 was an early attempt to redress the flagrantly inhumane living conditions the city had come to tolerate.[2] Such laws enforced a new minimum: all living spaces must have windows open to the exterior (Fig. 4). With that one Act of the legislature, whole city blocks of windowless slums were rendered illegal.

In 1916, the first complete zoning code collected individual laws into a vision of the city. There were now not only requirements for livable light and air but also new rules on bulk and the minimum size of courtyards used for windows.[3] Limits on height and setbacks from the street sought to preserve daylight into the city's thoroughfares. Along with the building code, minimum sizes of courtyards and the distance between buildings allowed for ventilation and light for living spaces, but also preserved fire separation between buildings. Each new law was a covenant linking the interests of a single property to its impact on the city as a whole.

But the zoning code has become more than just a snapshot of a moment at the time of its inception. It has been amended and updated endlessly. Some amendments responded to increasing density, reflecting anxieties about the city's shape and character. Buildings getting too big or too tall triggered Floor Area Ratio, linking the amount of building to its site area.[4] Rather than a cohesive vision or even a set of priorities, the zoning code has come to reflect the complexities of the city itself, each update making adjustments, adding asterisks, contingencies, and exceptions. While the 1916 zoning code

2   New York State Tenement House Act of 1901.

3   City of New York Board of Estimate and Apportionment, Building Zone Resolution, Adopted July 25, 1916. Section 17. Courts defined minimum outdoor spaces permitted

for rooms in which "people live, work, sleep or congregate."

4   The 1961 Zoning Resolution in October 1960 added controls using floor area instead of only the Sky Exposure Plane along streets.

was 12 pages, by 2018 the text was more than 1,300 pages long.[5] Many additions still strive to conceive of the city as a whole. And yet with each update, the exponential layering of requirements further obscures its promise as a vision of how we all live together.

***

Zoning codes, mazes of interwoven requirements, often come with unintended consequences. Some simply reveal the difficulty in creating laws that compel desired outcomes, while others unintentionally create opportunities for innovation.

The requirement of windows opening to the exterior that drove the invention of light shafts has evolved into a now-ubiquitous thirty-foot (ca. nine-meter) requirement for open space outside of every legally required window in a living space, either into the street or into a courtyard of a minimum size.[6] Although the spirit of the law is to undo the inequity of dark and dank tenements, in practice the distinction between "legally required" light and air and actual light and air can be unexpected.

Courtyards with irregular shapes and portions less than thirty feet in any direction aren't permitted for legally required windows.[7] Recessed into courtyards deeper than they are wide, as well as small courtyards less than ten feet (three meters) in any direction and below 200 square feet (18.5 square meters) aren't permitted at all, even as both these scenarios could add supplemental windows (in addition to legally required ones) for

5   NYC Planning, *Zoning Handbook,* © 1990, 2006, 2011, 2018 (New York: Department of City Planning, 2018).

6   This requirement is a combination of requirements from the zoning code and the building code. The zoning code defines distance required outside legally required windows in ZR 23-861, while the building code defines requirements for natural light in Section 1203 and ventilation in Section 1205.

7   See New York City Zoning Resolution, Section 12–10, "Court Recess, Inner."

Fig. 4: Tenement-house plans, from before the first tenement law was passed to the gradual integration of various light shafts (highlighted in gray).

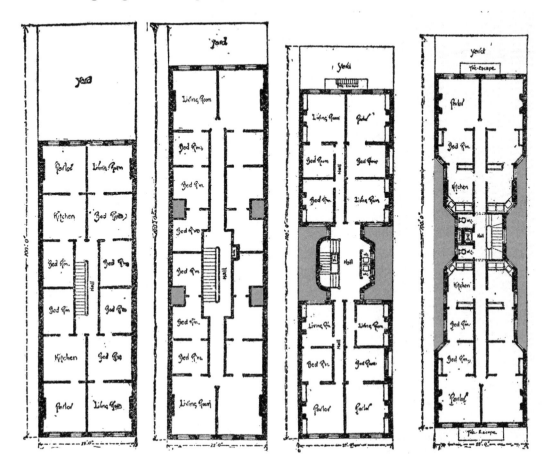

Fig. 5: Many existing buildings, including a large portion of the current housing market, were constructed before the introduction of the 1916 Zoning Resolution. Highlighted in black – buildings currently occupied that were built between 1894 and 1916.

cross ventilation.[8] Of course, the spirit of the code is to prevent inhumane living conditions with little or no access to light and air. And yet the strict dimensional requirements often result in courtyards needed for legally required windows being made smaller, chopping off those portions that don't meet the thirty-foot minimum, and eliminating altogether courtyards below the minimum size.

These are not the only unlikely outcomes of the zoning code. That the zoning code changes over time means that whole parts of the city were built under different versions in the code's development (Fig. 5). Manhattan's East Village and Brooklyn's Bedford-Stuyvesant neighborhoods, for example, were largely built under the 1901 New Law guidelines that permitted small light shafts between buildings for light and air, but which certainly do not comply with current guidelines. If we collectively decided these smaller light shafts were so inhumane, why do we allow these existing buildings to be grandfathered in as legal living spaces? A significant share of the city's current housing stock was built before the first 1916 zoning code added stricter light and air requirements.[9]

A surprising result: new and old codes now compete in the same housing market. The code changes triggered by Riis's images were not designed to protect land value, but they may be doing just that. Unlike the nonconforming housing now grandfathered in, new construction is governed by much more onerous requirements, such as thirty-foot light and air and minimum room and dwelling-unit sizes. A similar-sized lot now can accommodate fewer units and is subject to stricter laws. What began as laws to protect the interests of the city's lowest-income residents have strangely created new development with significantly more light and air than the smaller, more

8 See New York City Zoning Resolution, Section 23–851, "Minimum Dimensions of Inner Courts."

9 Source: Morphcode http://io.morphocode.com/urban-layers/; accessed August 5, 2024.

affordable housing that still populates the city. Instead of a right protected by the city for all, thirty feet of light and air have again become a luxury for those who can afford it.

Although the code started out protecting living conditions in the city, it also limits how architects think about living in the city with different types of courtyards, even if furthering the ambitions of light and air. Instead of thinner, lighter, more porous buildings, with greater access to light and air using supplementary courtyards that might not meet minimum dimensions, the code perversely incentivizes deep blocks with double-loaded corridors.

The zoning code's many-layered rules and complexities also offer unexpected opportunities. Code requirements defined in more flexible terms create necessary limits while leaving room for innovation.

With limits on floor area came floor area "deductions" – concessions that do not count toward limits when in the service of a greater good. For housing, an especially interesting deduction is open outdoor space. Its broad incentives encourage balconies, roof terraces, and exterior covered areas. The rule is simple: a perimeter at least 33 percent open. Unlike the light and air parameters which require certain dimensions, this kind of guideline leaves much more room for invention while being easy to demonstrate compliance.[10]

Exploring outdoor space for housing presents many opportunities. Rather than cantilevered balconies that feel peripheral to living spaces, we have created balconies and terraces pulled within the building envelope, treated more like outdoor rooms that extend indoor living areas. Meeting the rule, these

10   See New York City Zoning Resolution, Section 12–10, "Floor Area" (10).

90

Fig. 6: 450 Warren uses deductible outdoor-space rules to provide many generous outdoor rooms and a fully exterior network of bridges that connect apartments. None of these spaces (highlighted in gray) counts toward the allowable floor area.

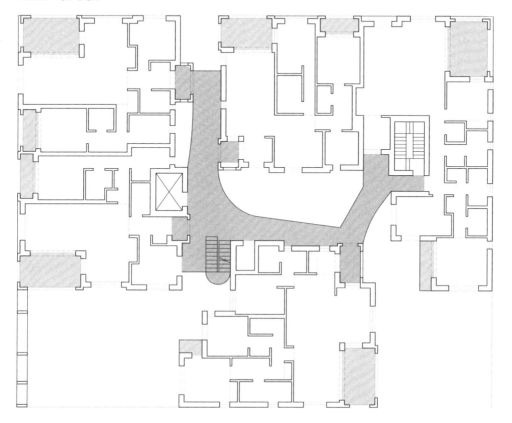

are deductible. Instead of glass guardrails, we use solid balustrades for small balconies off bedrooms to act as privacy buffers from the street: a garden outside your bedroom. In place of enclosed corridors and elevator lobbies, these can be exterior too, now light and airy outdoor spaces. Each of these reinterprets an element of the housing puzzle using deductible outdoor space as an incentive (Fig. 6).

Instigated by outdoor-space deductions, each front door opens directly to sun or rain. Balconies can extend and supplement indoor spaces, blurring indoors and out, all without counting toward maximum floor area. If more of the code were written with simple tests like this, it might easily go back to being a framework for invention instead of sameness. A code to encourage balconies becomes a way to propose new ways of living.

Codes are often memorials to past failures rather than templates for future goals. But in these rules, there can also be immense opportunity for invention. Each parameter the code limits or incentivizes might be the next thesis for a new approach to living.

The zoning code is just one of the codes that governs the conception of the city. The energy code is another.[11] Like the zoning code, the energy code has both an overall objective – to reduce energy consumption – and proposed prescriptive measures intended to achieve that goal. Like the zoning code, these prescriptive rules don't always result in the best way of achieving the goal. Working around the energy code is not a suggestion that we shouldn't take its goals seriously, but rather that our obligation extends beyond the letter of the law to inventing new strategies that further its larger objectives. Put simply, there are ways of reducing energy use besides the ones the code incentivizes. The energy code is designed to compel performance but is generally prescriptive in its ap-

11   The New York City Energy Conservation Code (NYCECC).

92

proach. Baked into this framework are assumptions of an ideal building that meets its goals. But this ideal building might not actually make an ideal place to live.

Despite the fact that the energy code and the zoning code coexist, there are incentives from one code that contradict the objectives of the other. One example is the energy code's objective of making buildings as airtight as possible. This means conditioned air stays inside and unconditioned air stays out, and heating and cooling systems have less work to do. And yet the best airtight building is not necessarily the best building in other ways. Perversely, the best building from an airtightness standpoint would have few windows that residents never open. What the building code calls "light" and "air" (both good), the energy code calls "solar heat gain" and "air leakage" (both bad). If only the windowless tenement houses Riis photographed were better insulated, they might be ideal buildings from the perspective of the energy code.

Interestingly, the energy code does also allow for a performance compliance path through energy–cost modeling, which offers an alternative to the architectural implications of the code's prescriptions. For those projects willing to invest in greater engineering costs, this allows projects with atypical energy strategies a way to show compliance. Even if not frequently used (yet), this introduces a valuable foresight of flexibility into the code that the zoning code lacks.

Taking a performance path, new metrics help measure the impact of architectural strategies on user comfort and building performance. Architecture should shape how spaces fundamentally change our relationship to energy use. Rather than applying new technologies to old ways of living, measuring the performance of architectural strategies pairs innovative systems and inventive spaces. Using metrics, a number of architectural strategies show that energy efficiency and livability can go hand in hand.

Fig. 7: 144 Vanderbilt – Net Energy Cost Savings strategies as compared with the code minimum.

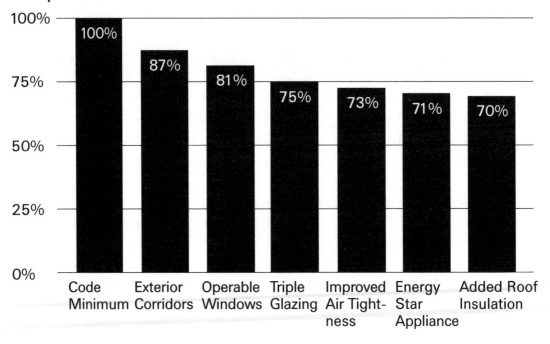

Fig. 8: 144 Vanderbilt circa spring 2024.

Fig. 9: 144 Vanderbilt uses operable windows that face different orientations to promote passive ventilation.

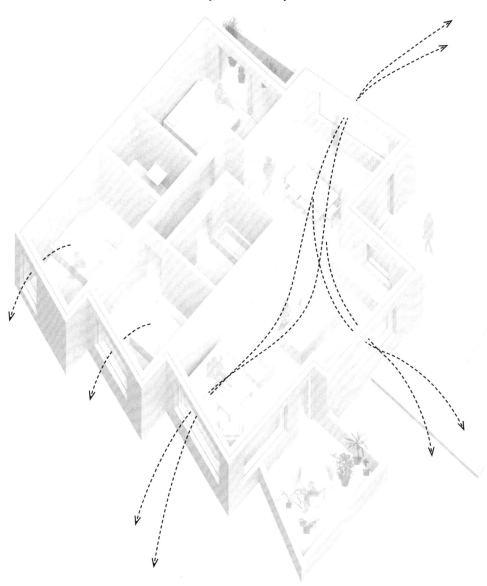

Exterior circulation is the first idea that couples these ambitions. Each apartment gets a front door that opens to fresh air and additional windows that encourage cross ventilation. Corridor space formerly within the thermal envelope no longer has to be heated or cooled. In one project, this strategy alone improved energy use by 12 percent above code minimum, more than using triple glazing, increasing the airtightness, using Energy Star appliances, and increasing roof insulation – all combined (Fig. 7). And yet the simple idea of reducing conditioned space is not incentivized anywhere in the energy code.

Another strategy is cross ventilation, using windows on opposite exposures. Operable windows encourage passive ventilation and don't rely on conditioned air during temperate months. In New York City, allowing residents to control cross ventilation reduced the number of days air conditioning might be needed down to a level that almost makes it unnecessary.[12] The potential energy saving was an additional 6 percent above code minimum, equal to upgrading all windows to triple glazing (Figs. 8, 9).

Of course, the code is not wrong in stipulating that airtightness is important, but it considers buildings as machines instead of living environments. People open windows when it feels good; the code should account for this. We should recognize that providing more ways to meet requirements would only encourage more compliance, not less.

***

The particularities of the zoning code and the energy code are specific to place as well as vision. Each is an evolving guide of everything the city hopes to incentivize and discourage, learned

12 Air that is moving as opposed to standing still shifted the range of comfort on the psychrometric chart into the range that no longer required air conditioning to achieve comfort for most days that had previously required air conditioning in the New York City climate zone. Analysis and data courtesy of Entuitive.

from past lessons. At the same time, we should recognize where those codes have started working against one another or where their prescriptiveness is incentivizing development contrary to larger goals.

One hundred thirty-four years later, the problems of density and livability that Riis brought to light are still very much unsolved, especially as the city struggles with record housing shortages. Our approach to these problems can't rely on the lowest common denominator between codes but should seek new shared ambitions. These codes structure buildings but also our cities. As the need for density grows and the stakes for codes become ever higher, we should encourage more flexibility in how their expectations are met. There should always be another way.

CANCEL THE CORRIDOR
NICOLAS KEMPER

"I was shocked to discover what sort of state is acceptable here," Florian Idenburg, co-principal and co-founder of the architecture firm SO–IL, tells me. I was talking with him about a New York design crutch that impoverishes residential living here by comparison with his native Netherlands: the double-loaded corridor (Fig. 1). What's the case against double-loading a corridor? "Well I would turn that question around and ask: can you tell me one thing going for double-loaded corridors?" says Sam Alison-Mayne, the head of the Brooklyn developer Tankhouse.

So called because rooms load onto them from both sides, double-loaded corridors are a problem for Alison-Mayne because of the light and ventilation they deny to the units they connect. Want an apartment with light from three sides? Cross ventilation? A balcony or a deck? If the building uses double-loaded corridors, then you better be ready to pay up for a corner unit or a penthouse. Idenburg emphasizes the lost potential of the connecting spaces themselves. As he wrote in a piece in *The Architect's Newspaper*, "Can we imagine the journey from apartment to street as joyous and celebratory, filled with daylight, fresh air, and lush plants? Not a furtive flight but a languid promenade, with spaces for repose along the way?"[1]

SO–IL and Tankhouse have gone further than imagining – they are building a series of double-loaded-corridor-free buildings in Brooklyn, beginning with the recently topped off 450 Warren Street. How do you get around without a double-loaded corridor? There are three main methods: puncture your building with circulatory courtyards (possibly wrapped with an

1   Florian Idenburg, "Op-Ed: When Health Crises Shut Down Urban Life, Domestic Spaces Should Fill the Gap," *The Architect's Newspaper*, October 20, 2020, https://www. archpaper.com/2020/10/op-ed-when-health-crises-shut-down-urban-life-domestic-spaces-should-fill-the-gap/; accessed August 5, 2024.

Fig. 1: The view from the author's front door: a double-loaded corridor.

Fig. 2: Balconies, light, cross ventilation: one floor of 450 Warren.

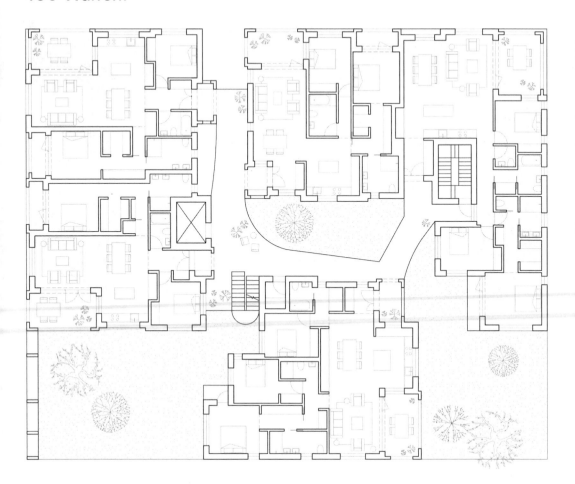

Fig. 3: A machine for stressful living. Circulation versus Living-Centered apartments adapted from the study by Sonit Bafna, Dr. Earle Chambers, and Herminia Machry.

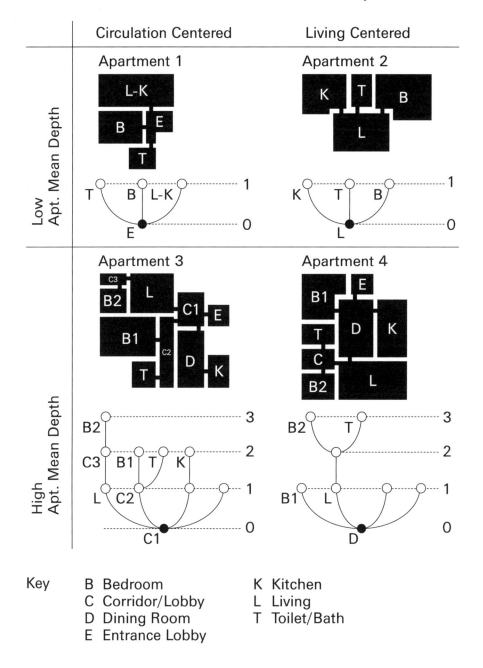

Key
B Bedroom
C Corridor/Lobby
D Dining Room
E Entrance Lobby

K Kitchen
L Living
T Toilet/Bath

arcade or single-loaded corridor), allow for direct circulation from room to room (upscale: enfilade; downscale: shotgun), or turn each unit into its own separate pavilion, forming together a campus, a solution embraced (with the exception of MIT) by older American colleges. At 450 Warren, Tankhouse and SO–IL are using a courtyard crossed by a series of curved, exposed walkways. Complete with trees, stoops, and the occasional bench, they connect the units to one another, all of which consequently receive light from three sides, have balconies, and enjoy cross ventilation. In this understated but wildly complex design, a unit owner will walk outside to access the elevator as though the street begins at their front door (Fig. 2).

The corridor's likeness to the street is what first enticed Dr. Earle Chambers, Director of Research in the Department of Family and Social Medicine Research at the Albert Einstein College of Medicine, to study apartment hallways and foyers (Fig. 3). He had been interested in the connections between the walkability of lower-income neighborhoods and the health of their inhabitants. Realizing that similar concepts used to measure walkability outdoors might also translate to indoor spaces, he received a $750,000 grant in 2010 from the John D. and Catherine T. MacArthur Foundation to look at the links between housing and the cardiovascular health of Latinos in the Bronx. Along with collecting health information from 371 low-income Latino families in the Bronx living in affordable housing, his researchers examined 291 units, diagramming room adjacencies, the doors connecting them, and noting the function of each room. The researchers then sorted the apartments into two categories: "circulation-centered," where rooms are connected by spaces designated almost exclusively for circulation (that is, corridors); or "living-centered," where rooms are connected via communal spaces, such as a living room or kitchen. The paper Chambers authored in 2018 with Dr. Sonit Bafna, an architecture professor at Georgia Institute of Technology, and architect Herminia Machry demonstrated that interviewees living in circulation-centered apartments

Fig. 4: Spontaneous sex written all over it. Charles Fourier's Phalanstère.

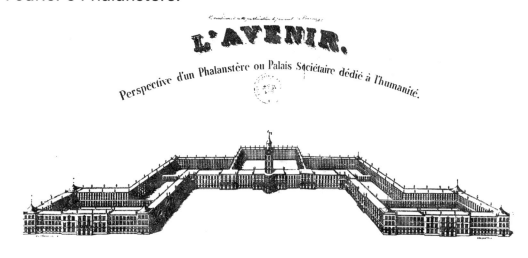

Fig. 5: Point blocks: a corridor-free plan in Singapore.

were significantly more likely to experience symptoms of depression. Why? The authors speculated the cause may be related to depth – the distance from private to social space. The more depth a layout has, the more socially isolated its inhabitants are – and social isolation can be, said the study, "a significant predictor of health problems," including stress.[2]

The possible connection to stress may be because corridors are often symptoms of a hierarchical social structure. That is to say, the first corridors were designed not by their users, but those who use their users. In his 2010 piece "Corridor Spaces," for the journal *Critical Inquiry*, architectural historian Mark Jarzombek writes that in the fourteenth century, *corridor* meant someone who runs fast, carrying the orders of commanders (later: courier).[3] Corridor took on an architectural meaning: "spaces in fortifications that enabled rapid communication with troops." That may be why, as Idenburg's partner at SO–IL, Jing Liu, puts it, stepping out into a hallway from an apartment can feel like being "ejected from your home." Widespread use began with barracks design – so much so that Germans would use the word *Barackenstil* to describe buildings with double-loaded corridors, such as schools and hospitals. Jarzombek emphasizes the class implications. Double-loaded corridors showed up in barracks, palaces, and institutions as spaces where the commanded can access their commanders without fraternizing.

Paradoxically, through its history, the double-loaded corridor also repeatedly played a starring role in utopian visions – perhaps because, again like a street, a corridor can be a space of potential spontaneity, surprise, and subversion. In his 2019 book *Corridors: Passages of Modernity*, Roger Luckhurst foregrounds

2   Earle Chambers, Sonit Bafna, and Herminia Machry, "The Association Between Apartment Layout and Depressive Symptomology among Hispanic/Latino Residents in Low-Income Housing: the AHOME Study," *Journal of Urban Health* 95, no. 1 (February 2018): 51–60.

3   Mark Jarzombek, "Corridor Spaces," *Critical Inquiry* 36, no. 4 (June 2010): 728–70.

the Phalanstère – a self-contained utopia that resembles a university or mental institution, and which centers around double-loaded corridors – designed by the French theorist Charles Fourier.[4] They were to facilitate not just spontaneous contact, but spontaneous sex. These utopian structures, writes Luckhurst, were intended "to dismantle all prior social relations, most particularly the bourgeois family, folded in on itself behind closed doors" (Fig. 4).

A good street privileges both movement and sex – well, it provides the sort of generous amenities (light, air, nature, a place to sit) that foster spontaneous interactions and, by extension, civil society. New York has been extremely intentional about its streets, to the point where the most stringent rules shaping buildings are rooted in maximizing the amount of light and air in the streets. Yet New York has had different priorities with its internal streets. The city is full of corridors without natural light or natural ventilation, much less plants or anywhere to sit. These corridors are not only legal but often, per building code, mandatory. Rules aimed at making fire stairs safe during a fire make them miserable places to be at any other time. The energy code, in turn, punishes a building for adding the extra envelope necessary for cross ventilation. A regulation receiving a lot of attention is the fire-safety mandate in North America that all buildings of a certain height have two means of egress. While there is little proof that the second egress actually improves fire outcomes, it is very clear that it incurs real costs: to have two egresses accessible from all units, there must be a hallway connecting them. "Single-staircase radicals," as Henry Grabar called them in a 2021 *Slate* article, are pushing

4   Roger Luckhurst, *Corridors: Passages of Modernity* (London: Reaktion, 2019).

5   Henry Grabar, "The Single-Staircase Radicals Have a Good Point," *Slate*, December 23, 2021, https://slate.com/business/2021/12/staircases-floor-plan-twitter-housing-apartments.html; accessed August, 19, 2024.

to reform building codes to allow for high-rise buildings with, well, a single staircase.[5]

Finally, the building code privileges conditioned – that is, heated and cooled – spaces. While these are well-intentioned rules aimed to keep inhabitants safe and warm, their consequence is, as Idenburg puts it, "everything that is unheated is chopped off, and what you are left with is a box." Idenburg points to a movement in Switzerland to heat only the rooms in which we spend significant time, such as the kitchen and living rooms, and leave everything else unheated. By contrast, "In the US there is the outside, then total control of the inside."

While Alison-Mayne bets the extra light and cross ventilation will sell units at 450 Warren, he sees Tankhouse's work, too, as beginning with streets, specifically the qualities of Brooklyn's streets and public spaces. Those qualities, like those of cities in the Netherlands, may have much to do with the simple lack of towers, and therefore the tendency of units to connect via open streets, not corridors. 450 Warren – and two more projects under way, one on Chapel Street in Dumbo Heights and another on Vanderbilt Avenue in Fort Greene – represent a test of whether those qualities can extend into high-rise living.

As a high-end development, it may be easy to write off 450 Warren as a high-end solution (units begin at $1.7 million), but SO–IL's earlier experiment with a double-loaded-corridor-free building – its 2012 competition entry, named tiNY, for adAPT NYC – focused on affordable housing. It placed micro-units on a seasonally open-air single-loaded corridor, such that each unit would have cross ventilation and receive light from both sides. In Singapore, code and a cultural aversion to double-loaded corridors makes them rare at any price point (Fig. 5). For the health and happiness of New Yorkers everywhere, hopefully city leaders here too can amend the building code to make our internal streets as good as our external.

LAYERED LIVES
KARILYN JOHANESEN

The building envelope transcends the conventional view of the facade as mere representational surface. Instead of a single boundary, the building envelope is composed of multiple layers, each influenced by particular regulatory, financial, and physical constraints.[1] These constraints restrict housing development in New York City by demanding neat delineations between home and community, private and public, and the conditioned and exterior climate. As a result, the majority of residential buildings in New York City feature envelopes that isolate residents from one another and the surrounding environment. Delaminating the layers of the building envelope reveals opportunities to reestablish connections between our homes and our city.

The outermost layer of a building envelope is constrained by the zoning envelope.[2] In his prophetic response to the NYC 1916 Zoning Resolution, *Metropolis of Tomorrow*, Hugh Ferriss describes the zoning envelope as a "shape which the Law puts into the architect's hands" and that, without a preconceived vision, the architect follows logical steps to mold it into a practical final form (Figs. 1–4).[3]

1   Recent theories of the building envelope – such as *The Ecologies of the Building Envelope: A Material History and Theory of Architectural Surfaces* by Alejandro Zaera-Polo and Jeffrey Anderson (New York: Actar, 2021); and *Nature of Enclosure*, edited by Jeffery S. Nesbit (New York: Actar, 2022) – challenge the established narratives around facade and surface by positioning the building envelope as a materialization of modernity's dichotomy between human and nature through an assemblage of social, political, and economic ecologies.

2   The NYC Zoning Resolution defines the building envelope as "the maximum three-dimensional space on a zoning lot within which a structure can be built, as permitted by applicable height, setback and yard controls."

3   Hugh Ferriss, *The Metropolis of Tomorrow* (New York: Ives Washburn, 1929).

Figs. 1–4: Illustrations showing the logical steps with which an architect molds the envelope into a practical building form. Hugh Ferriss, *Metropolis of Tomorrow* (1929).

Fig. 5: The Riverside Building, built in 1890, features exterior circulation.

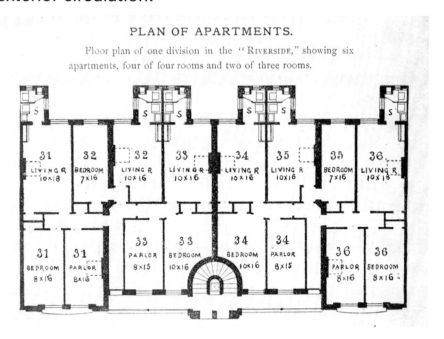

Fig. 6: The Riverside Buildings, seen in context.

The straightforward steps Ferriss outlined in 1929 have become significantly more intricate today – particularly for housing, where the spreadsheet has become the predominant force in shaping our living environments. Subsequent amendments to the zoning resolution such as height factor, floor-area ratio, open-space ratio, quality housing deductions, and affordability incentives have added more complexity to a matrix of ratios that pits zoning and code requirements against profit maximization. The pro forma demonstrates a project's profitability by establishing target efficiency ratios and allocating a construction cost per square foot based on comparable projects in nearby housing markets. The building envelope is assigned its own efficiency ratio, determining a cost per square foot, thus limiting the choice of envelope assembly early in the process. Within the complex framework of zoning regulations and the pressures of market-driven efficiency metrics, the envelope finds itself hemmed in: its boundaries are predefined before an architect can take any first logical step.

The innermost layer of a building is constrained by the requirements of the core. The core embodies all necessary flows through a building – people, energy, water, and gravity – and is primarily constrained by the Life Safety Code. That the core mainly exists outside of the sellable floor area means it is ruled by efficiency. But the core need not be relegated to the purely efficient shaft in the dark center of the building. By reexamining the core's relationship to the envelope, the journey from city to home can be enhanced without sacrificing efficiency. An early example of an exterior core and circulation in New York City is the Riverside Buildings in Brooklyn Heights, built in 1890 (Figs. 5, 6). Developed by philanthropist and housing reformer Alfred T. White as a solution to the squalid tenement conditions the working class were subjected to, the exteriorization of the circulation allowed two orientations of daylight and cross ventilation from the street to generous inner courtyards.

Fig. 7: The ubiquitous envelope assembly found in New York City housing reflects the pressure of regulatory and economic constraints on the envelope layers.

Fig. 8: Typical NYC apartment design with a central corridor providing access to units on both sides.

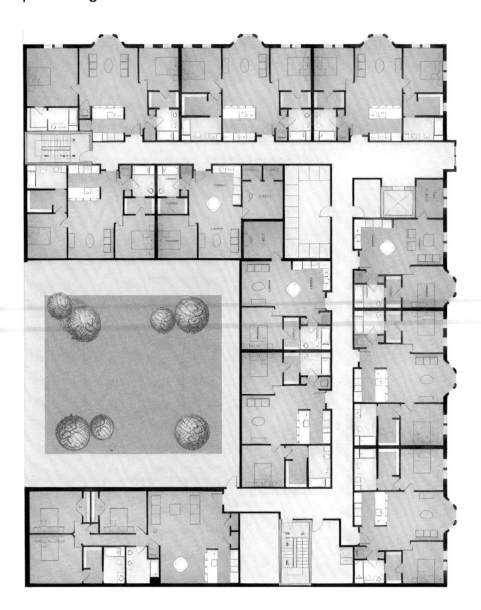

Between the zoning envelope and the core, the thermal envelope is the layer which performs the role of separating our home from the environment. The New York City Energy Conservation Code mandates that a single line can be drawn between inside and outside in order to calculate the energy efficiency of a building. A shorter line with fewer punctures achieves a more efficient envelope. As the imperative of envelope efficiency ascends to the forefront of architectural priorities, it paradoxically fosters a disconnect, insulating our immediate living spaces from the surrounding environment that demands our stewardship.

While the capacity for an envelope assembly to keep rain and wind out is nonnegotiable, its thermal performance has historically been in flux with a direct correlation to the cost of energy. Rising energy costs, coupled with an attuned awareness of buildings' contribution to global climate change, have prompted regulation to increase the minimum energy performance, which has resulted in increased insulation thickness. The thicker envelope assembly conflicts with the profitability of gross-to-net floor-area ratios. Despite the introduction of a floor-area deduction for envelopes that meet higher energy performance, thinness remains a virtue.[4]

With its high insulation value, relative thinness, and at nearly half the cost of other envelope systems, EIFS (Exterior Insulated Facade System) has prevailed as the dominant envelope assembly for housing projects in New York City. Commonly paired with a masonry or panelized rainscreen at the street-facing facade, the remaining building envelope – including

4   The "Zone Green" amendments, introduced to the Zoning Resolution in 2012, aimed at promoting green building by eliminating regulatory obstacles. These amendments included a provision that permits the deduction of a portion of the exterior wall thickness from the overall floor-area calculations on the condition that the building's thermal-envelope performance exceeds the Energy Code's stipulated requirements by a certain percentage.

Fig. 9: Bulkheads, balconies, dormers, and street wall articulations erase the dominance of the zoning envelope in determining 9 Chapel's building volume.

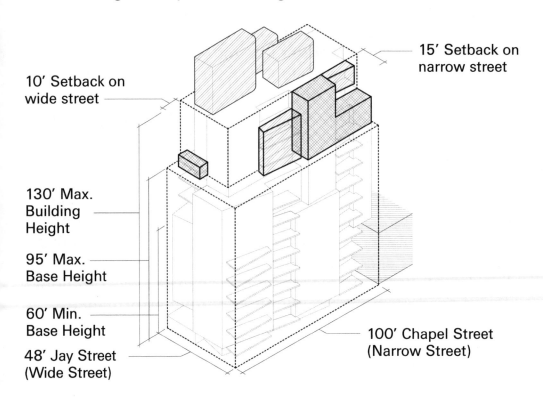

15' Setback on narrow street

10' Setback on wide street

130' Max. Building Height

95' Max. Base Height

60' Min. Base Height

48' Jay Street (Wide Street)

100' Chapel Street (Narrow Street)

▭ Permitted Dormer
▭ Permitted Balcony Obstruction
▭ Permitted Bulkhead
▭ Adjacent Building
‑‑‑‑‑‑‑ Zoning Envelope

Fig. 10: Rotations in plan create pockets of outdoor space at 9 Chapel, while the excavated core creates a protected elevator lobby with front porches on either side.

Fig. 11: 9 Chapel's room-scale articulations erase the dominance of the zoning envelope. The building envelope steps away from the sidewalk and neighboring structures to create more generous entries.

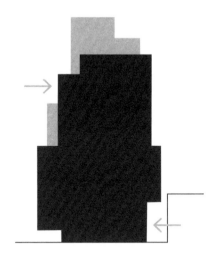

party walls, court- and yard-facing facades, setbacks, and bulkheads – homogenize into the smooth, jointless surface of EIFS (Fig. 7). The distribution of budget toward a single face of the envelope is indicative of the regulatory and economic environment in which housing operates in New York City. To meet the target efficiency ratios, the thermal envelope is pushed tight to the zoning envelope while presenting an image of luxury only toward potential customers.

Upon entering a typical New York City housing building, the pursuit of efficiency ratios narrows the movement of residents into streamlined shafts and double-loaded corridors, constrained by their disconnection from the city and the monotonous repetition of generic unit entries (Fig. 8). Zoning setbacks allow for ample outdoor spaces, but only for the few inhabitants at the top. When outdoor space is allocated at lower floors, it frequently manifests as inhospitable balcony extensions. Different metrics are needed in which ratios do not dominate over spatial qualities, such as access to generous outdoor space for all units, multiple orientations of daylight and ventilation, and diverse interactions with the surrounding context along the journey from city to home.

9 Chapel, a twenty-seven-unit condominium project in Downtown Brooklyn, serves as a case study in delaminating the layers of the building envelope. The rigid boundary that separates home from city is pulled apart into multiple layers, creating spaces in between where a diversity of experiences and interactions can flourish.

The outermost layer of the building envelope is blurred and softened by breaking down the zoning mass into the scale of individual rooms. Subtle rotations and shifts between bedrooms and living areas pull the thermal envelope away from the zoning envelope, forming pockets of outdoor space (Fig. 9). Taking advantage of the compact site and vertical zoning envelope, the towers of rotated rooms, some indoor and some

Fig. 12: Exterior circulation at 9 Chapel provides additional outdoor space to each unit as a front porch.

Fig. 13: A unifying veil wraps 9 Chapel, while a variously curved masonry inner layer creates depth and texture.

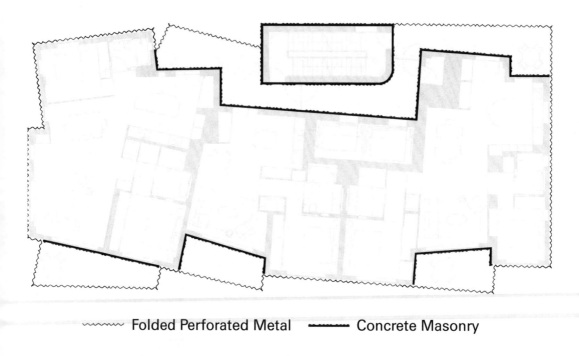

Folded Perforated Metal ▬▬▬ Concrete Masonry

Fig. 14: Three panel types are rotated and mirrored at 9 Chapel to create combinations of curves and sharp folds which is the same from the inside as it is from the outside.

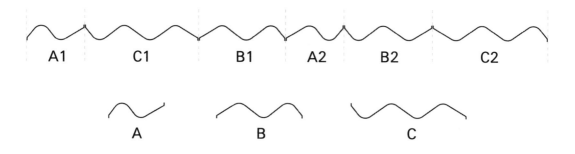

outdoor, mean that every unit benefits from multiple orientations, cross ventilation, and a variety of exposures to daylight (Fig. 10). These articulations and the use of other permitted zoning obstructions – including bulkheads, balconies, dormers, and street wall articulations – erase the dominance of the zoning envelope in determining the building volume (Fig. 11).

On the lower floors, the setback inverts, creating a permeable base for the building that steps away from neighboring structures. The thermal envelope is pulled back from the property line, revealing a sunken garden beneath the building mass above. Following the subtle topography of the sidewalk, the terraced zones buffer the shared amenity spaces and create intimate entrance experiences on two levels.

As in the Riverside Buildings of 1890, the shared circulation is external. The interior stair core is pulled out of the main building volume, sheltering the elevator lobby and dividing the exterior circulation routes into intimate pockets of space that become the front porches for each unit (Fig. 12).

The concept of delamination is reinforced at the scale of the detail, where the layers of the envelope assembly are revealed to create texture and depth that complement and extend living areas. Both the interior and exterior volumes are wrapped in the same pleated and perforated metal veil (Fig. 13). On the interior volumes, the veil functions as an open-joint rainscreen system, with black-faced mineral-wool insulation behind. On the exterior volumes, the veil shelters portions of terraces from unmitigated exposure to sun and wind, and creates a more intimate outdoor environment even high above the street. Using the structural logic of corrugation, the pleated panels span from floor to floor without the need for additional substructure.

The pleated texture combines curves and straight segments in three panel types that are rotated and mirrored to create an undulating texture with no front or back (Fig. 14). The texture of the panels from the inside of a terrace is the same as from outside. This inner envelope of variously curved masonry block contrasts with the transparency and lightness of the outer veil. The curves and folds of contrasting materials enhance the depth and layering of the envelope through an interplay with light and shadow.

From the scale of the building in the city to the material detail assemblies, the process of delaminating the layers of the envelope can begin to transform regulatory, economic, and physical constraints into opportunities for connection – chance encounters with neighbors, filtered experiences of climate and ecology, and unexpected interactions between the sanctuary of home and the life of the city.

Generous terraces and large windows make up a porous envelope

Dappled light trickles in from the side yards

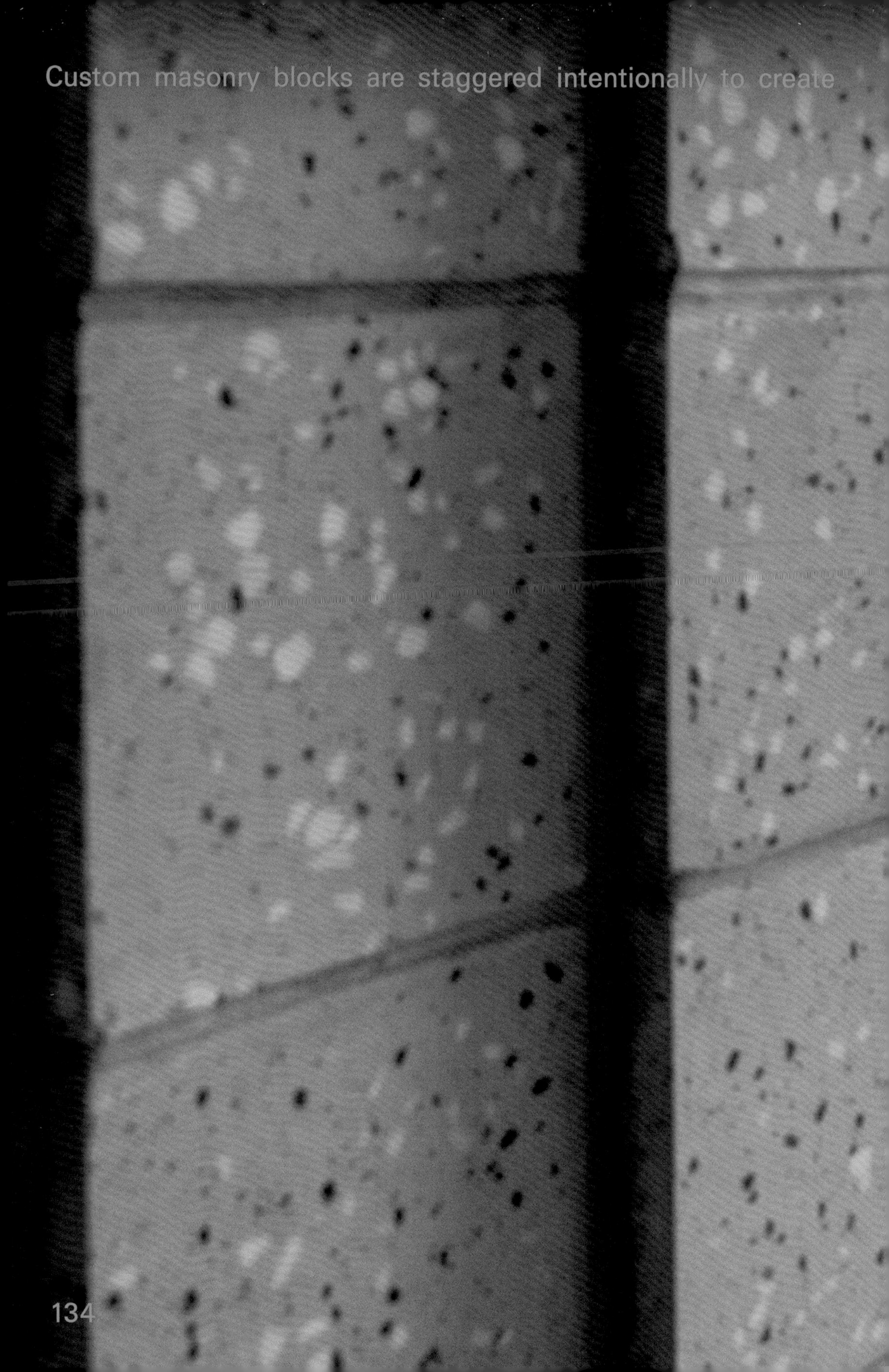

Custom masonry blocks are staggered intentionally to create

a deep texture throughout

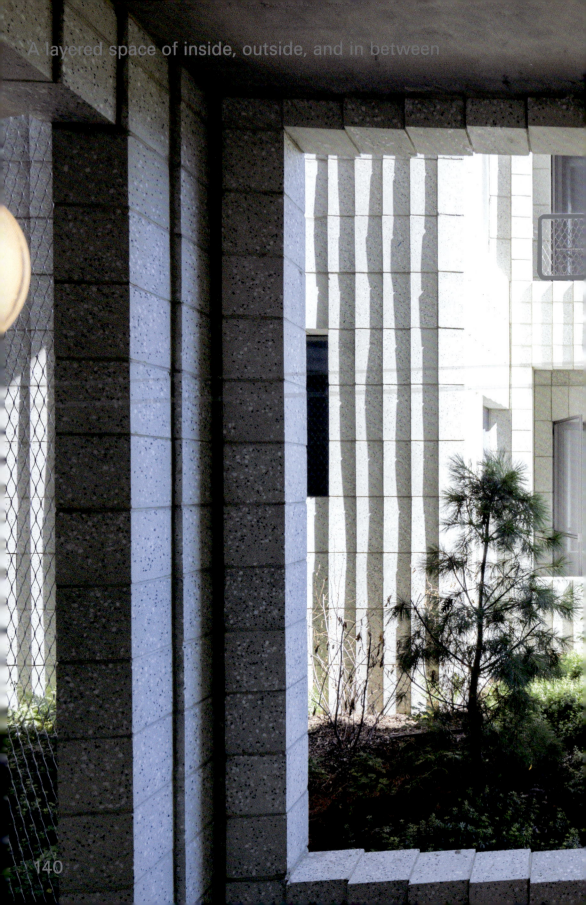

STANDPIPE
CONNECTION
INSIDE

A spacious, shared side yard

the Downtown Brooklyn skyline

155

Side yard, from above

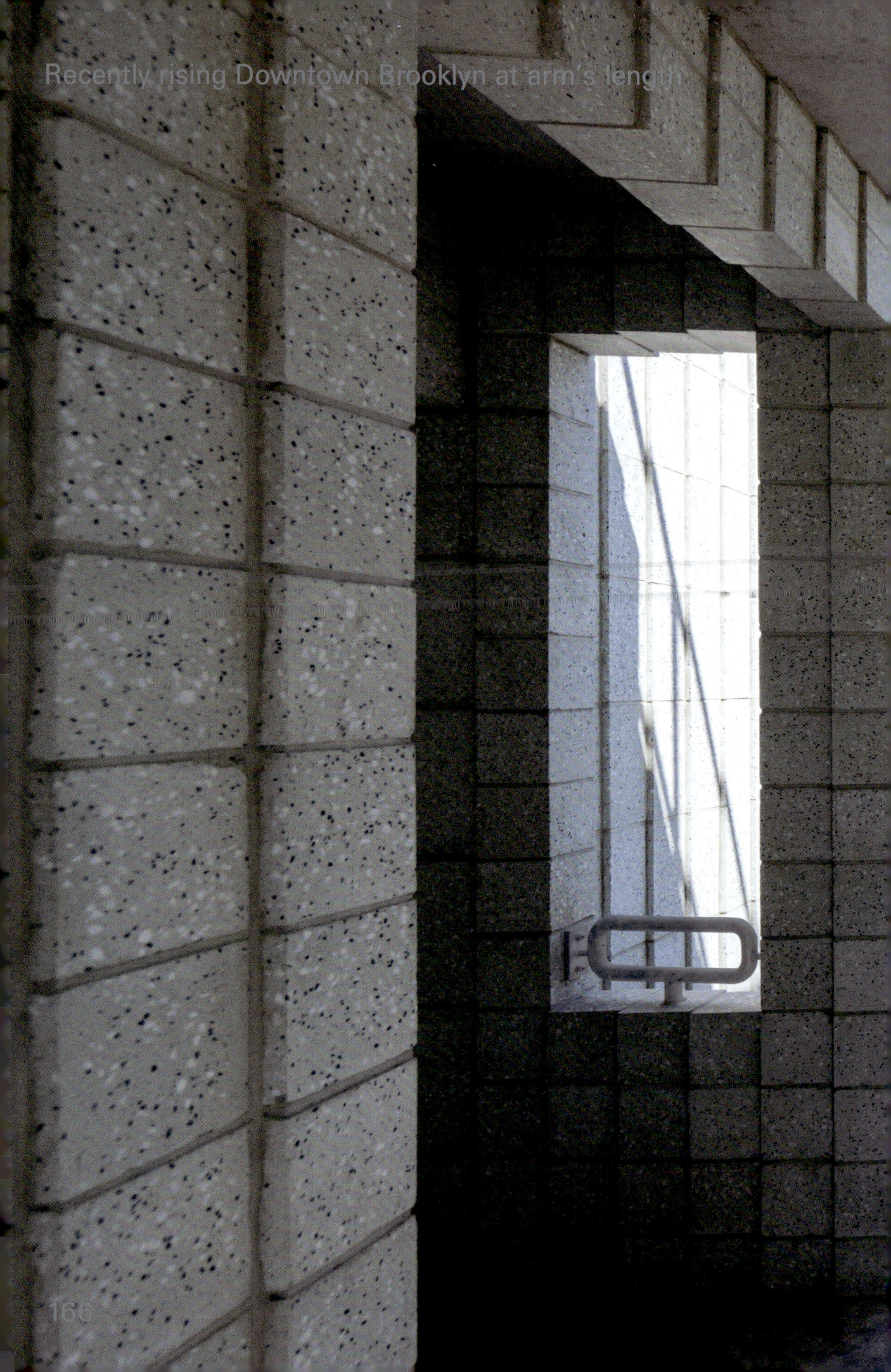
Recently rising Downtown Brooklyn at arm's length

PROJECTS

Cores: Breathe, Bergen, Clifton, 9 Chapel
Courts: Party Wall, PetalHouse, Adelphi, 450 Warren
Corridors: tiNY, Las Américas, 144 Vanderbilt, 450 Union

BREATHE
MILAN, ITALY

Conceived as a radical response to restrictive practices in urban housing design, Breathe models a circular, diffusive exchange between a dwelling and its environment.

Eschewing traditional layouts, Breathe unfolds as a series of porous, interconnected spaces. A modular steel frame is cloaked in a light-permeable, air-purifying fabric, which mediates between the indoor environment and the outdoor climate with minimal intervention. The seven-zoned structure blurs the lines between private and communal, expressing an open domestic narrative.

Designed for urban infill sites of only 50 square meters, Breathe is mobile and adaptable, supporting a dynamic living space for up to three people. The project proposes a sustainable, nomadic paradigm for city habitation, transforming the dwelling from a static series of walls to a living entity.

Isometric

Site Plan, 1:1,000 ☉

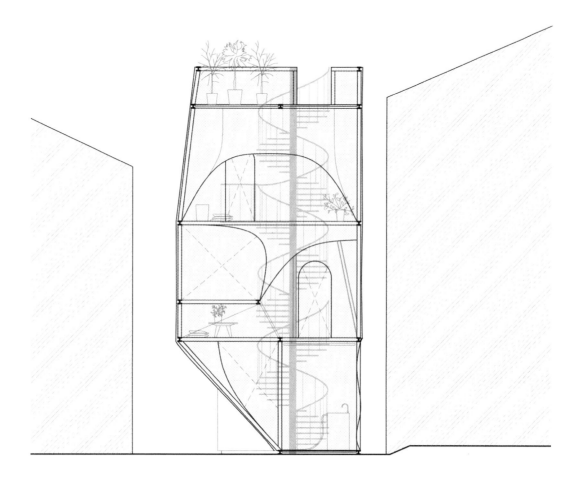

Third-Floor Plan, 1:100 ☉

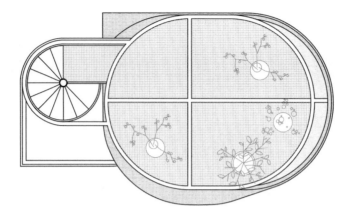

Second-Floor Plan, 1:100 ☉

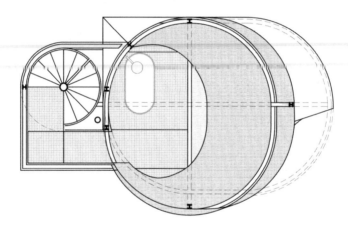

First-Floor Plan, 1:100 ☉

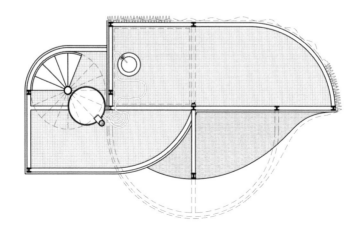

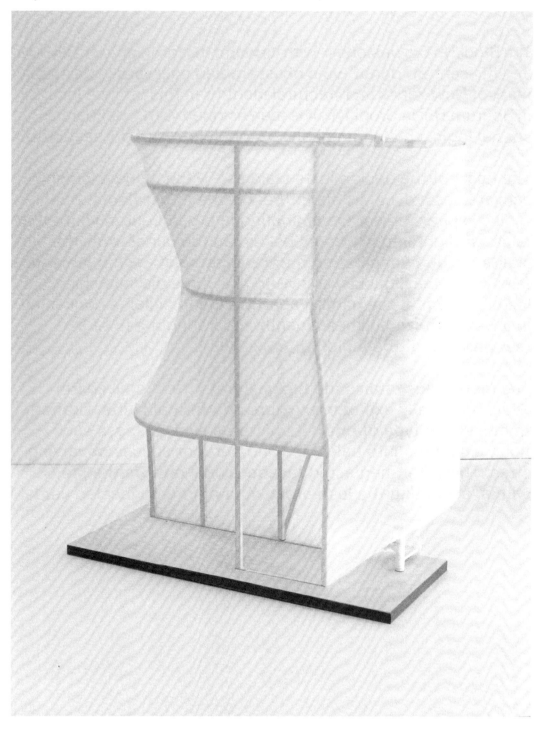

BERGEN RESIDENCE
BROOKLYN, NEW YORK, USA

The Brooklyn brownstone – with its warm masonry, efficient layouts, and the central "donut" void of assembled backyards – is a hallmark of New York's architectural identity. In this project, located in Boerum Hill in Brooklyn, it is reenvisioned with a deliberate spatial logic, challenging conventional norms of domesticity.

The heart of the design is its staircase, a functional element activated as a dynamic sculpture. On the upper floors, this "spine" spirals upward, culminating in a generous skylight that pours daylight into the floors below. On the parlor level, the stair splits in two, creating a transversal relationship between family members, guests, and visitors. A more discrete spiral leading down to the garden apartment and cellar is concealed in a Duchampian bulkhead, gently separating the front and rear portions of the building.

The rear facade retains the brownstone's traditional charm while maximally exploiting texture and formal shifts. Crafted from a single type of brick, its patterns evolve across each floor, extending into balconies and outdoor spaces of varying sizes. This often-neglected facade vividly mirrors the life within, animating the lush urban void of interconnected yards.

Isometric

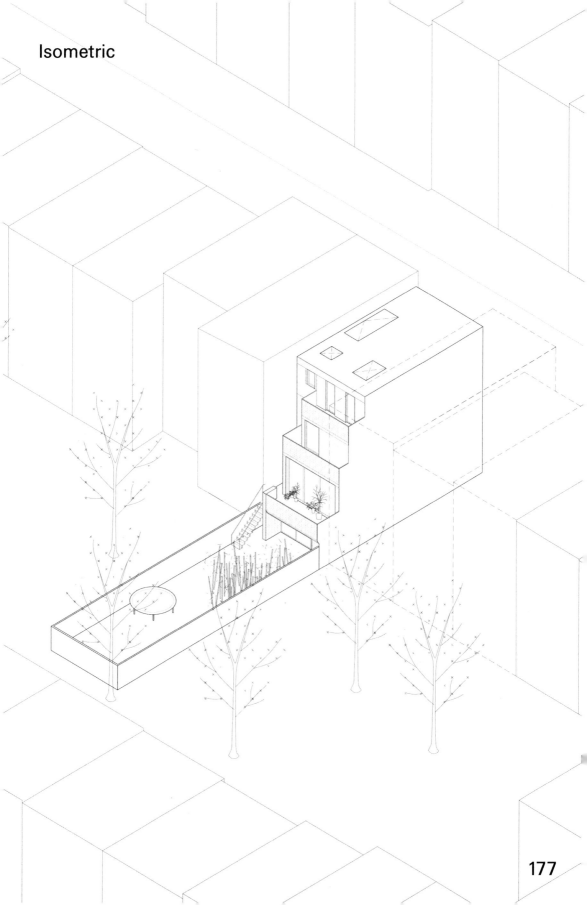

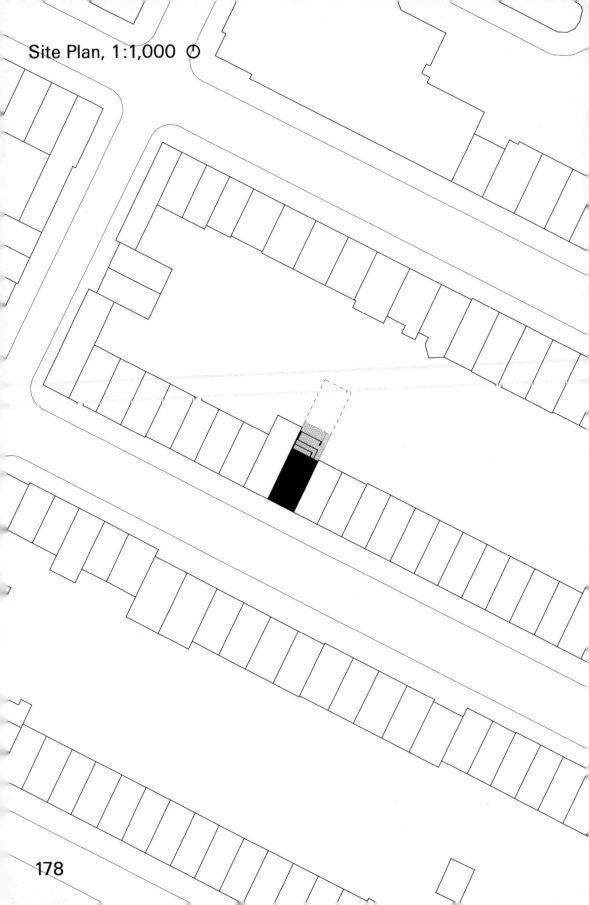

Section, 1:250

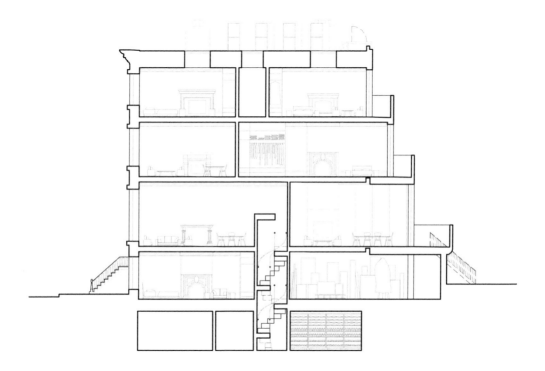

Garden-Floor Plan,
1:250 🕐

Elevated Ground-Floor Plan,
1:250 🕐

First-Floor Plan,
1:250 ⏱

Second-Floor Plan,
1:250 ⏱

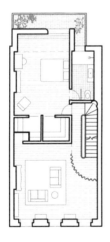

CLIFTON ARTIST HOUSE AND STUDIO
BROOKLYN, NEW YORK, USA

An artist's studio, office, and residence in Brooklyn's Clinton Hill adds two stories to an existing structure, weaving her work and life into a vertical spatial system.

Our design simultaneously regulates and stimulates the relationship between the expressive and quotidian facets of the artist's life. Inspired by the textures of her childhood home of Brazil, the building is executed in a simple, solid cinder block arranged in subtly shifting patterns, resulting in a playful and robust facade expression. Long slit windows allow daylight to permeate the street-facing side while maintaining privacy along the urban thoroughfare. A south-facing roof terrace, anchored by an oversized communal table at its center, allows daylight into the studio below.

In the interior, original floor surfaces are left as they are, composing a tapestry of textures alongside newer finishings. New structural bracings are intentionally framed diagonally and painted in a viridian green, breaking from the orthogonal and repetitive order of the everyday.

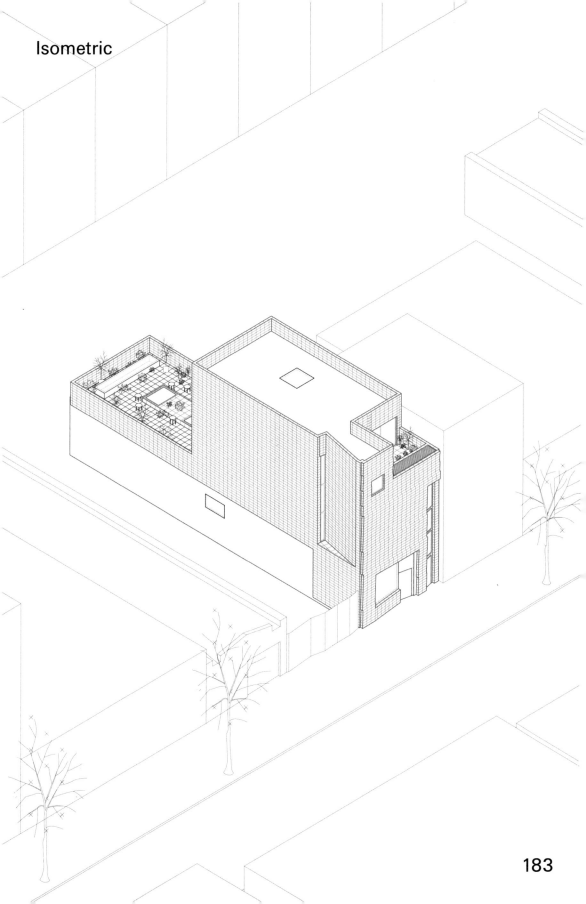

Site Plan, 1:1,000 ☉

184

Section, 1:250

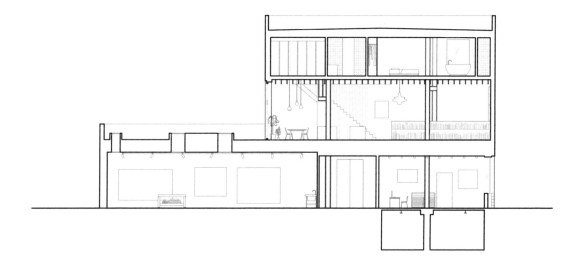

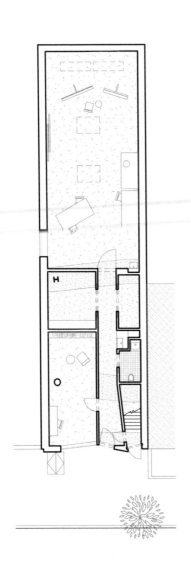

Study Model

Study Model

9 CHAPEL
BROOKLYN, NEW YORK, USA

With its unique four-sided exposure, 9 Chapel skillfully negotiates and integrates with its complex urban conditions. Adjacent to a basilica and an urban park in the Dumbo Heights neighborhood of Brooklyn, zoning constraints prompt the relatively small building mass to take on an expressive, fluctuating form. Built over a subway line, the building is elevated at ground level. An interlocking vertical entrance sits within a sunken communal garden, welcoming residents home into a quiet urban oasis.

The fourteen-story building is structured around a covered, unconditioned central core. Each floor offers a diverse array of irregularly assembled apartments, carefully rotated and oriented to take in varied city views and optimal daylight. The apartments are surrounded by a mix of outdoor spaces – balconies, terraces, front porches, and window gardens – expanding living spaces outward.

The exterior facade's perforated metal veil offers protection and privacy to the outdoor living areas, with an inner facade of raw structural concrete intermittently lined with custom cementitious blocks. This exchange between outer delicacy and inner robustness blurs the indoor–outdoor divide, heightening the building's depth and residents' cohabitation with an ever-changing environment.

Site Plan, 1:1,000 ⊙

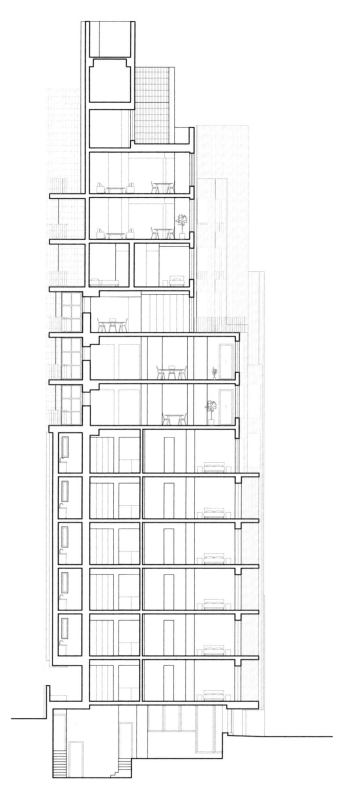

Typical Floor Plan, 1:250 ⊙

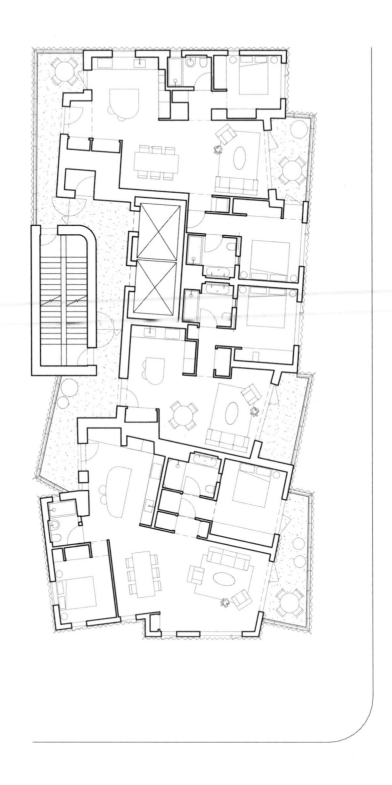

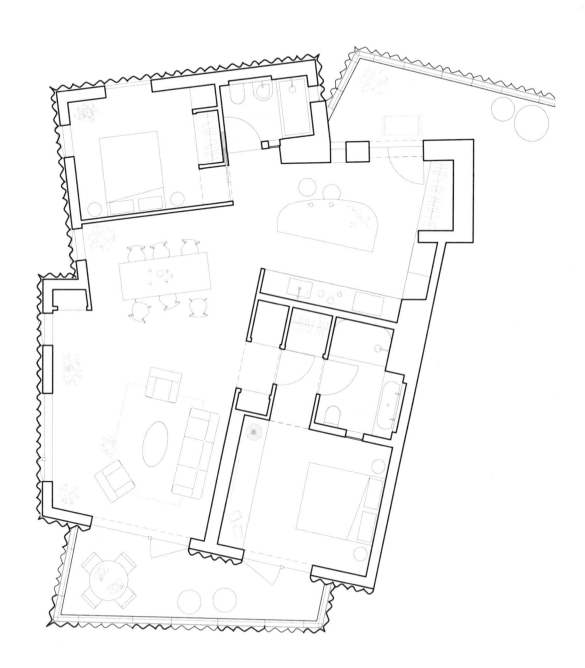

Physical Model

Physical Model

PARTY WALL
ATHENS, GREECE

The districts of Kerameikos and Metaxourgeio in Athens are characterized by a potpourri of building types, with closed, muted facades facing narrow streets. Backyards are often left dirty, unused, and out of sight. Party Wall proposes a student-housing prototype that shifts the building mass to one side, creating a series of 4.5-meter-wide side yards. City life becomes an integral part of the living experience, as a generous vertical circulatory space allows the kaleidoscope of student life to spill out from compact interiors.

This porous concept is designed to be applied to infill lots throughout the neighborhood, knitting together over time to form an interconnected network of social spaces offering daylight, intimacy, and city views. This strategy extends the spaciousness of the interior while also introducing density to the neighborhood. Layered spatial qualities, from focused and private on the inside to shared and social outside the front doors, allow students to shift between these modes quickly during this dynamic phase of their lives.

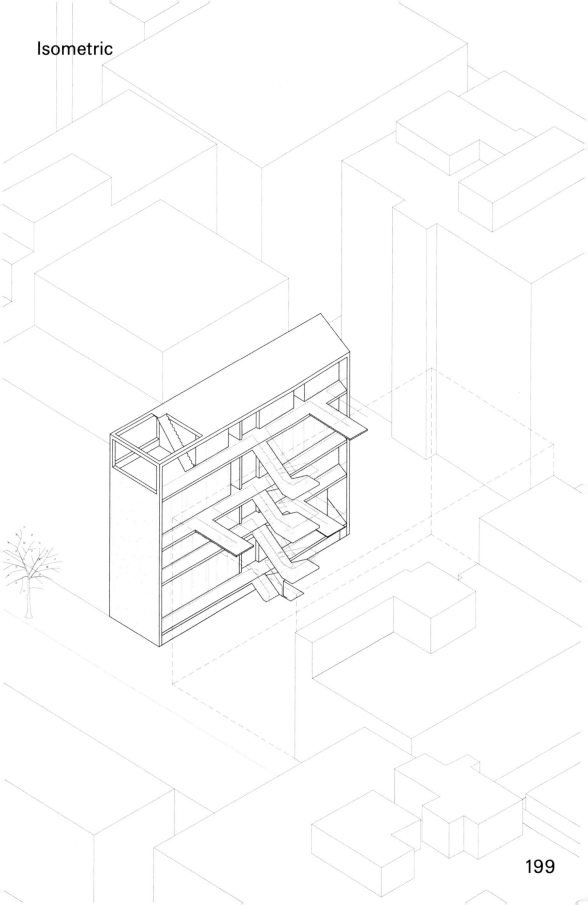

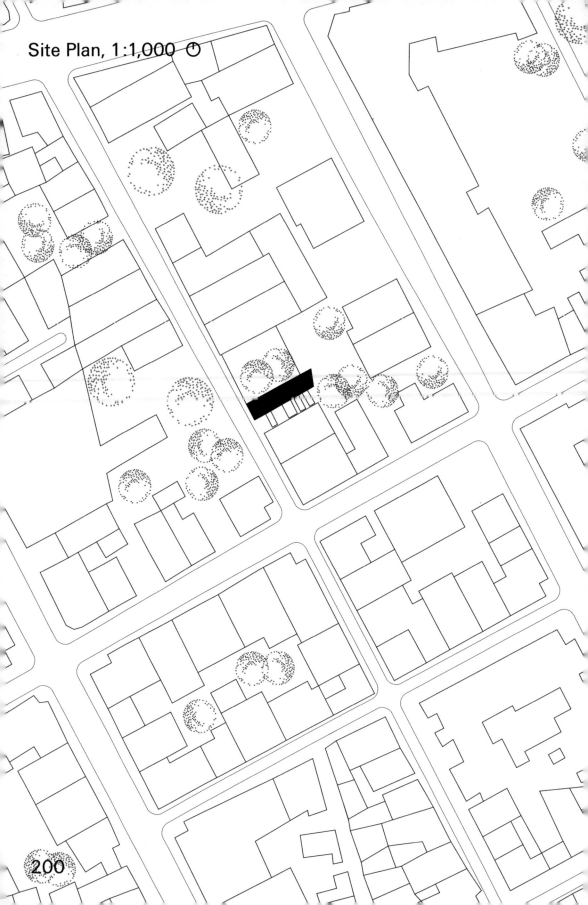

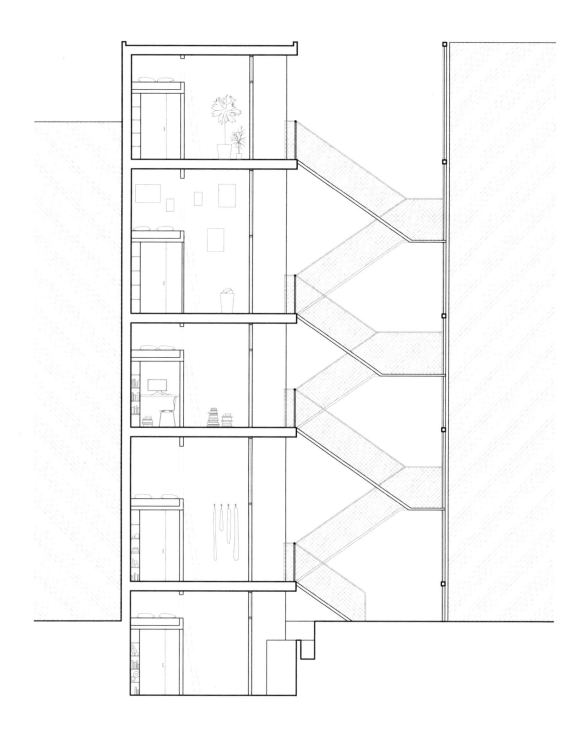

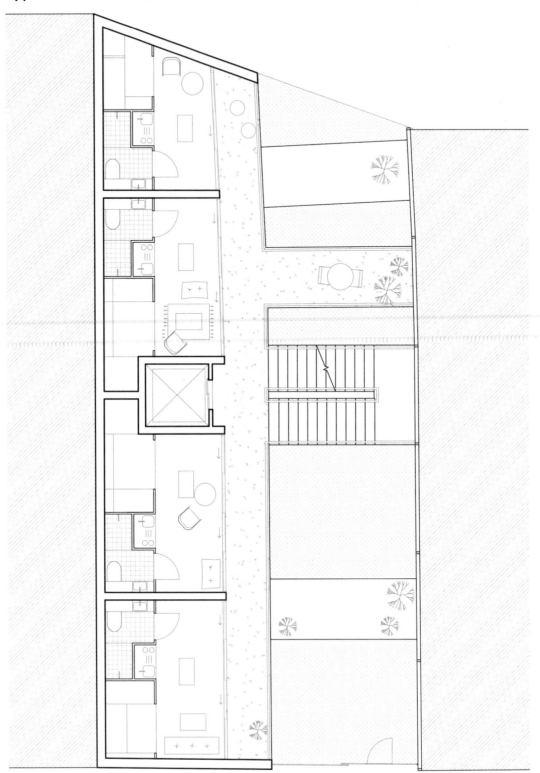

Physical Model

Physical Model

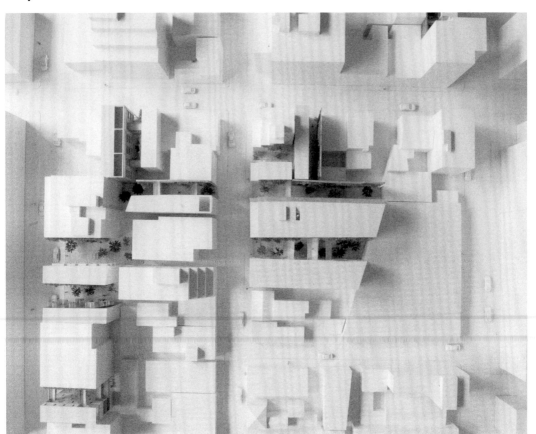

Physical Model

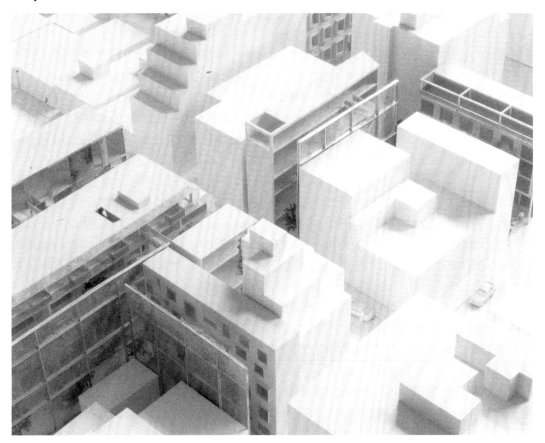

PETALHOUSE
LOS ANGELES, CALIFORNIA, USA

PetalHouse is an ADU, or Accessory Dwelling Unit, a residential dwelling unit constructed on a lot with a proposed or existing primary residence, providing complete independent living facilities for one or more persons. The design was developed as part of the Standard Plan Program of the Los Angeles Department of Building and Safety in 2020.

PetalHouse is inspired by Los Angeles's storied history of experimental homes and Case Study Houses, channeling a spirit of optimism and openness into exploratory dwellings. The house perches on a deck, its flower-shaped plan maximizing exposure on all sides. All mechanical and wet spaces are packed in an efficient core, liberating perimeters and allowing daylight and occupancy on all sides. The floor and roof extend beyond the facade, creating a shaded and elevated area for outdoor living.

PetalHouse's structure is made from cross-laminated timber, with a floor and ceiling composed of epoxy-coated wood. Its ability to be prefabricated off site and quickly assembled on site minimizes material waste as well as construction impact on the neighborhood.

Isometric

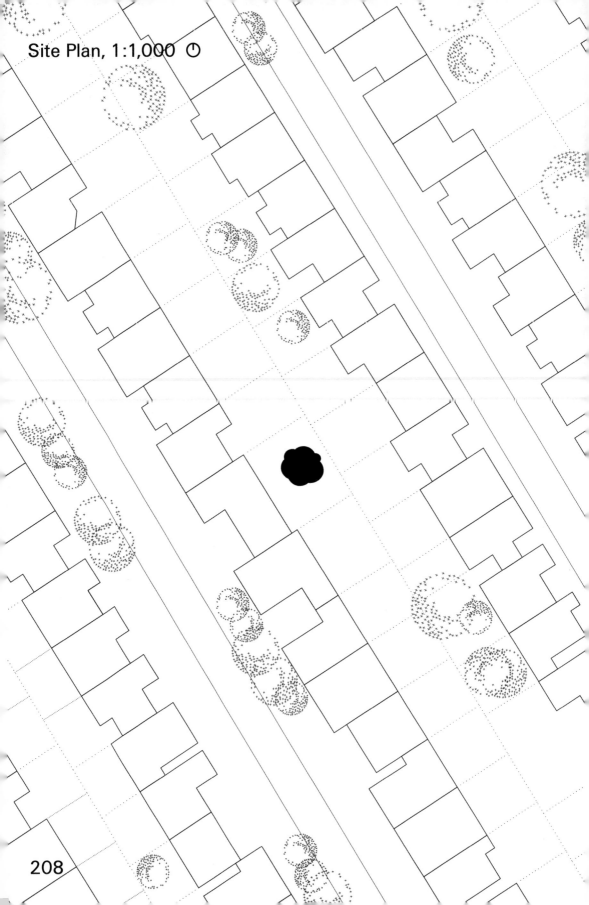

Site Plan, 1:1,000 ☉

Section, 1:100

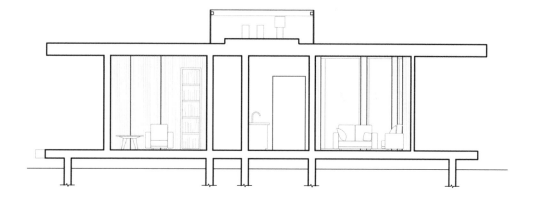

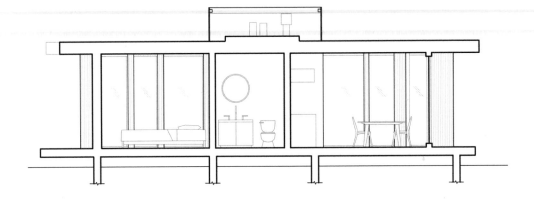

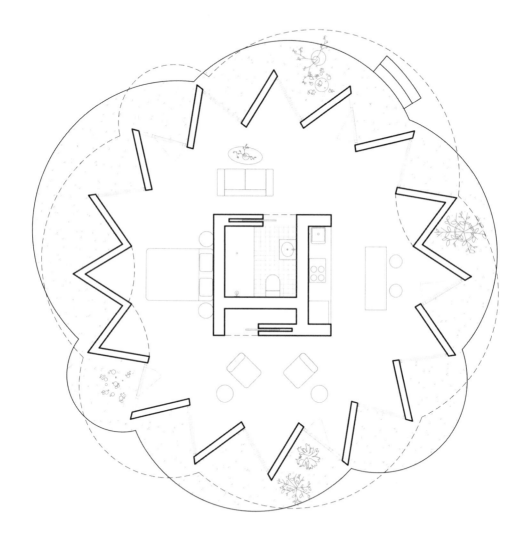

Physical Model

Physical Model

ADELPHI
BROOKLYN, NEW YORK, USA

Situated near the Brooklyn Navy Yard, a century-old carriage house has undergone a complete renovation, meeting passive-house standards while inviting ample daylight to the interior. Adjacent, a new office building of two double-height units is added, with a small alley between serving as an entrance to both.

The ground floor of the office space features a series of glass accordion doors facing the alley and garden that integrate the workplace with the outdoor environment. The open, versatile space accommodates a range of activities, from social gatherings to performances to gallery exhibits. A bookshop, communal kitchen, meeting room, and model workshop round out the main workspace. The top unit fills with natural light from clerestory windows, while views out to a rooftop garden provide a tranquil setting for focused work.

The office building's facade experiments with impregnated concrete canvas, typically deployed in civil construction. Its pillow-like texture softens the exterior, departing from the rational, unitized expression of office buildings. The project stitches together urban living, working, and leisure, balancing activity with tranquility and public engagement with private retreats.

Isometric

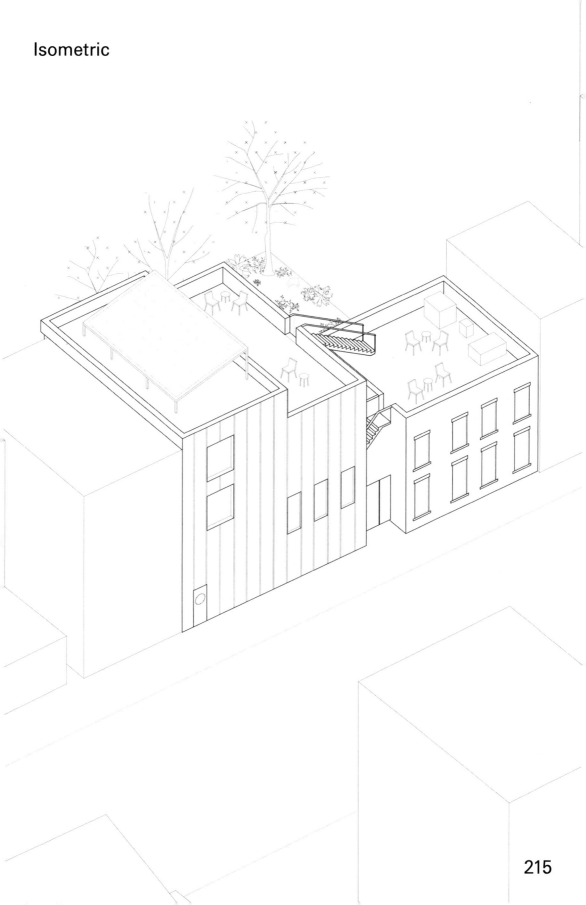

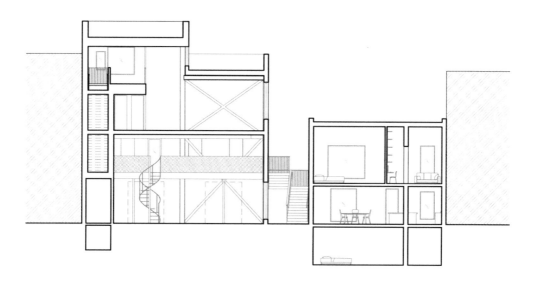

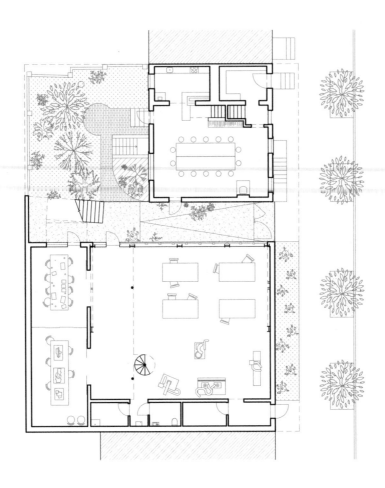

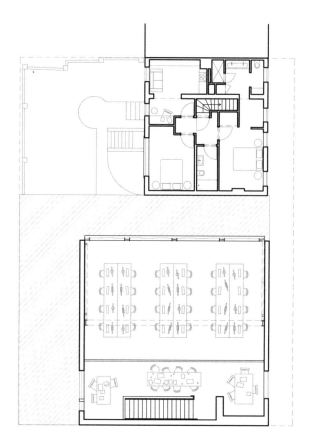

450 WARREN
BROOKLYN, NEW YORK, USA

450 Warren is situated on the edge between the historic brownstones of Boerum Hill and the postindustrial Gowanus Canal in Brooklyn. Bracketed by NYCHA social housing, it redefines the boundaries of these diverse neighborhoods through a dense, green, and robust urbanity. With its eighteen homes, this unique building breaks away from conventional multiunit apartment designs, emphasizing livability through interaction with both nature and community.

Occupying a corner site, large terraces and balconies connect the urban and the domestic along its porous perimeters. At the center, a sculpted courtyard surrounded by covered exterior stairs and corridors provides each apartment with its own direct exterior entry. These transitional zones, reminiscent of the Brooklyn stoop, extend the living space outdoors and provide opportunities for informal interaction with neighbors, blurring the line between communal and individual. Two additional landscaped side yards allow light, airflow, and greenery deep into the site.

Each apartment is afforded at minimum three exterior exposures, animated by the lush side yards, playful courtyard, and surrounding context. The facade's layered, textured masonry casts shadows that shift with the sun. Metal mesh enveloping the inner court and exterior walkways engages with the seasons, ensuring the building's rhythm stays attuned to the natural environment.

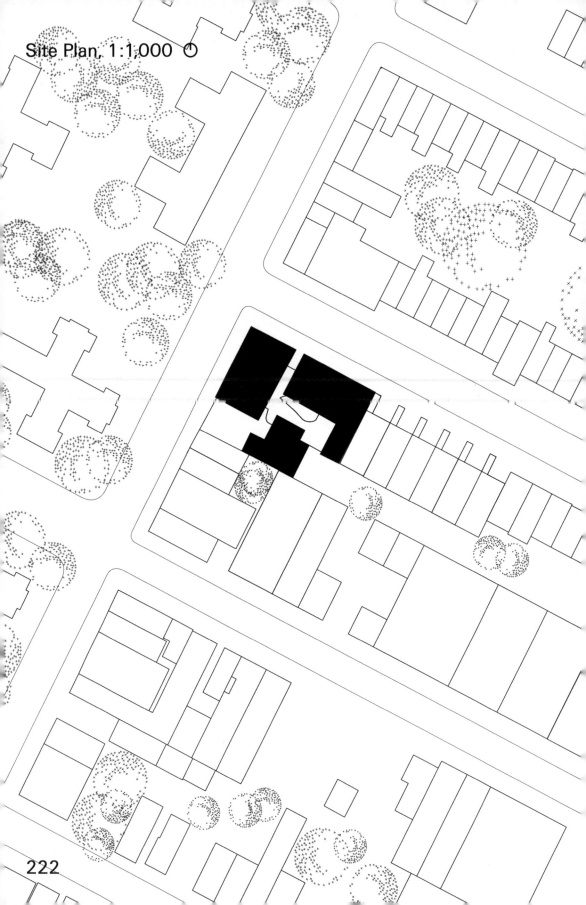

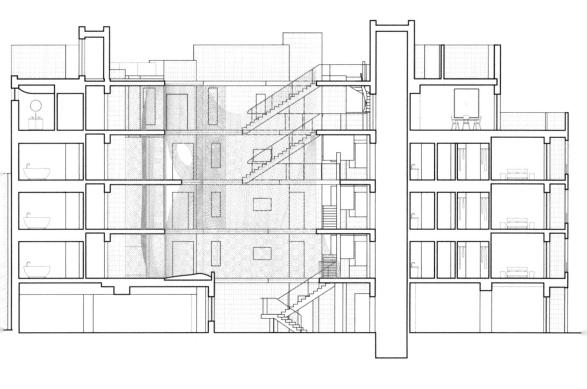

First-Floor Plan, 1:250 ⊘

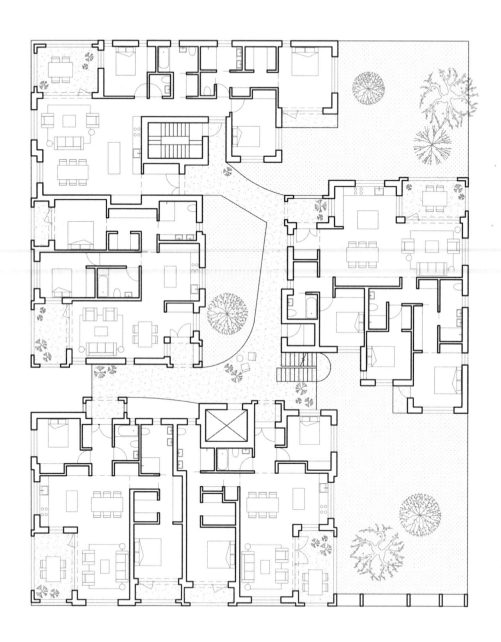

First-Floor Unit Plan, 1:100

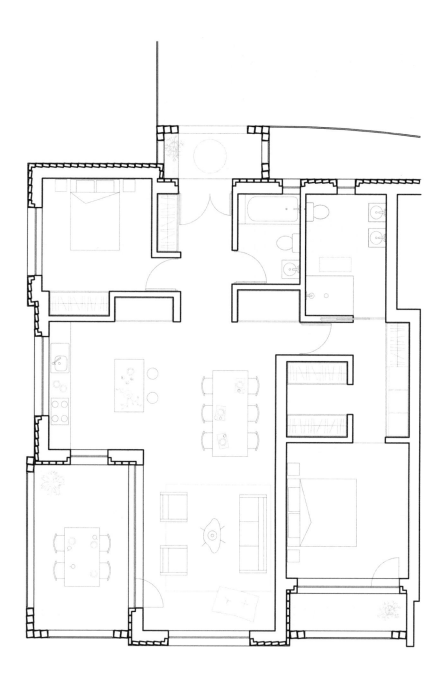

Physical Model

Physical Cutaway Model

Physical Model

Physical Cutaway Model

TINY
MANHATTAN, NEW YORK, USA

In 2012, New York Mayor Michael Bloomberg initiated adAPT
NYC, a pilot program to create a new housing model for
affordable micro-unit apartments. Our project, tiNY, located on
1st Avenue, between 27th and 28th Streets, presents a
unique response to this initiative, aiming to achieve affordability without the aid of tax incentives by capping developer
profits and using market demand to subsidize units within
the development.

Our design showcases this concept through a single-loaded
corridor on one facade connecting ninety-six micro-units
with private balconies on the opposite side, expanding the 22-
square-meter apartments. This layout redefines compact
urban living spaces, offering floor-to-ceiling windows, ample
daylight, cross ventilation, and accessibility in each
unit, with enhanced connection to the outdoors thanks to
an adjacent park.

tiNY is crowned with a common rooftop garden for its residents. At the street level, amenities such as bike storage
and repair shop, coin laundry, and temporary office spaces are
open to the surrounding communities, adding small but
much-needed improvements to the neighborhood.

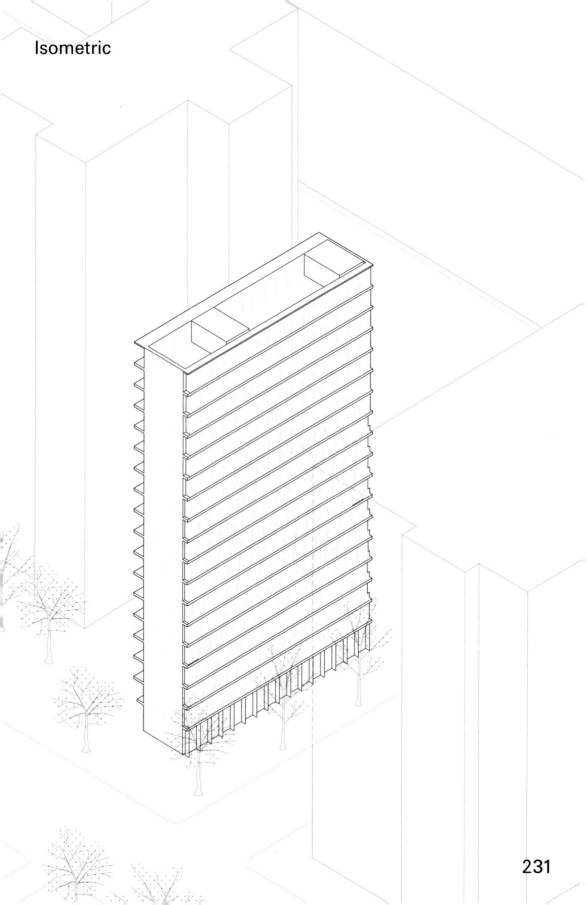

Site Plan, 1:1,000

Section, 1:250

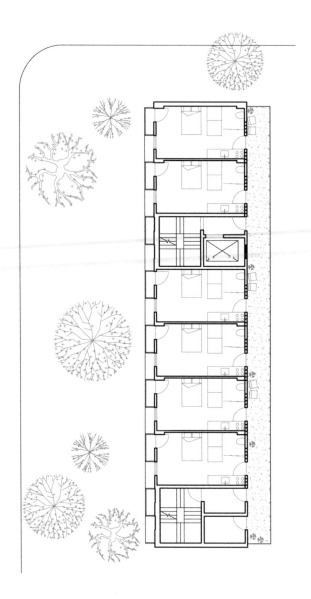

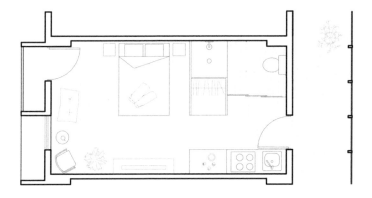

Physical Model

Physical Model

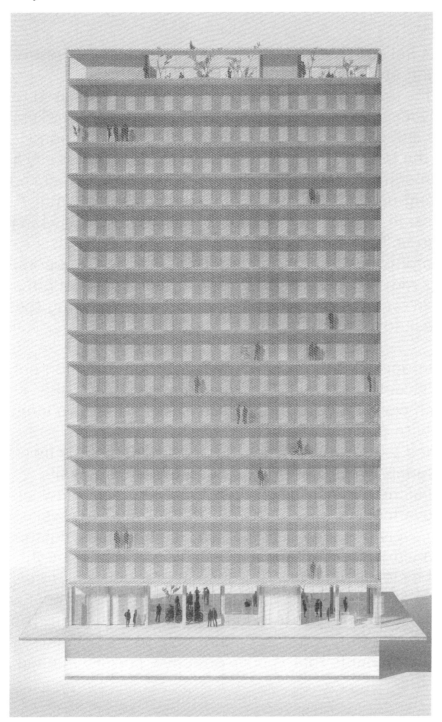

LAS AMÉRICAS
LEÓN, MEXICO

Las Américas in León, Mexico, serves as a prototype for vertical urban living in a city combating rampant urban sprawl. As much of the world's automobile manufacturing relocated to the industrial areas of Guanajuato state droves of migrant workers arrived in its cities. As one of its main municipalities, León has become the fastest-growing metropolis in Mexico. The city's expansion through low-rise, self-built neighborhoods has reduced density, putting pressure on municipal utilities and transportation systems. In contrast to traditional housing models, which often result in uniform detached homes in distant suburbs, this project proposes a dense building closer to the city's core. Collaborating with IMUVI, León's housing authority, we sought to spark urban renewal inside its inner city while enhancing the quality of life in low-income areas.

Our design integrates fifty-six 2- and 3-bedroom units on an empty lot adjacent to a market, school, and park. The building's layout efficiently utilizes available land, enclosing two inner courtyards, with parking and commercial spaces at the base. Designed to preserve privacy, no apartment directly faces another, fostering a sense of private homeownership. Units are arranged along a generous corridor that meanders between the homes, overlooking the courtyards which provide cross ventilation to every unit. The building's facade features a custom-designed concrete block, fabricated locally and light enough to be carried by local workers without special equipment. Intentional layering of these blocks creates a distinctive architectural expression, both on the interior and from the outside. The resulting building offers a unique alternative to traditional suburban developments that is cost-effective, socially minded, and sustainable.

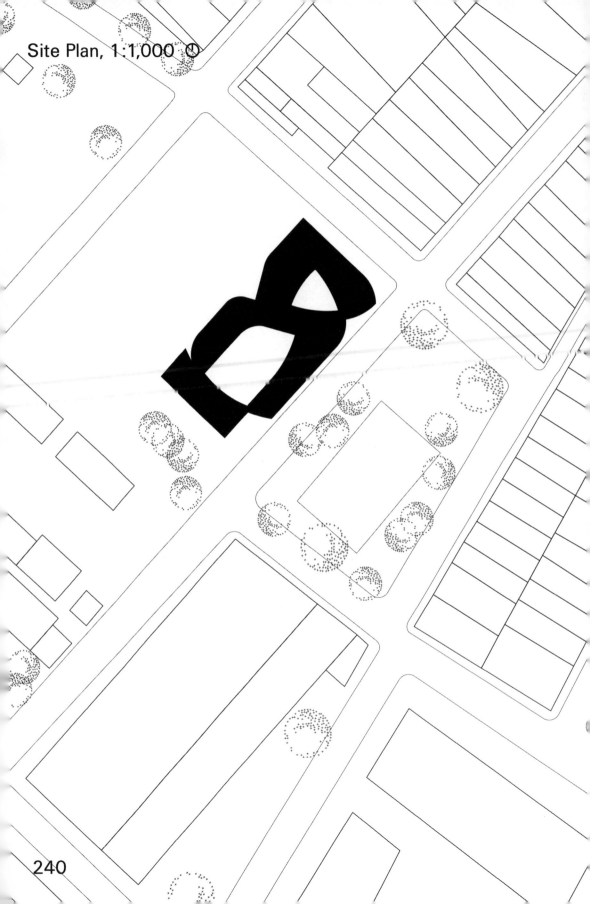

Section, 1:500

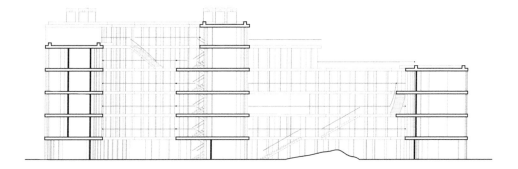

Typical Floor Plan, 1:500 ⊘

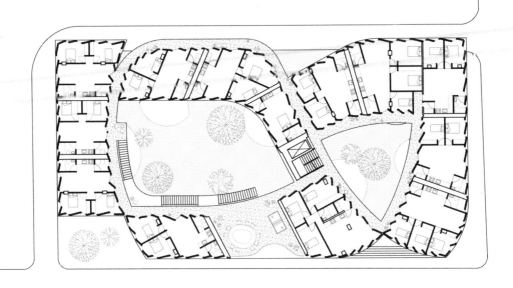

Unit Plan, 1:100

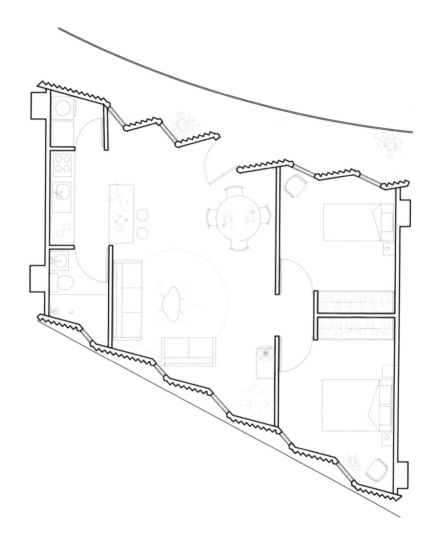

Study Models

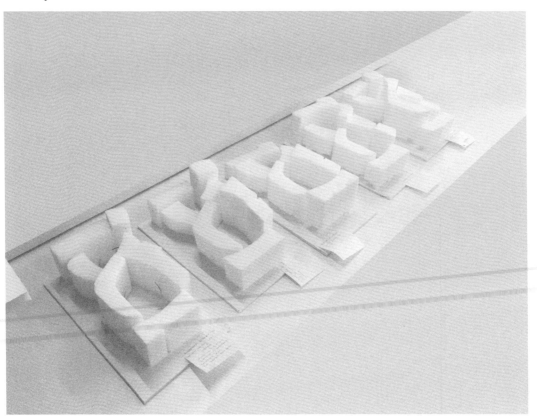

Physical Model of Selected Form

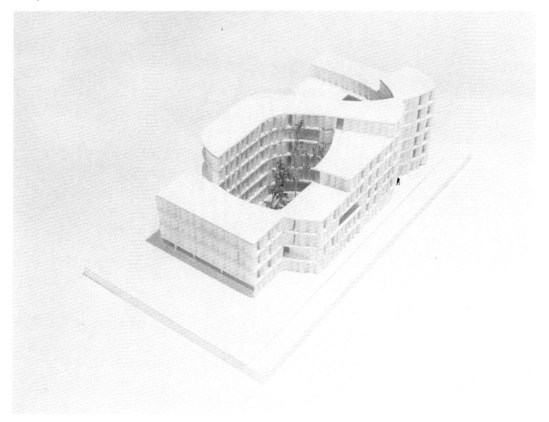

Presentation Model

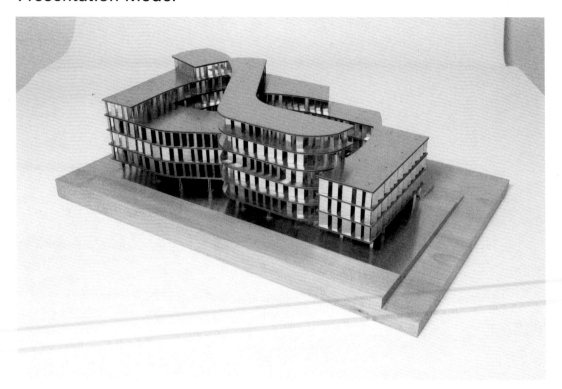

Presentation Model

144 VANDERBILT
BROOKLYN, NEW YORK, USA

144 Vanderbilt represents the third installment (after 450 Warren and 9 Chapel) in a series of residential buildings aimed at transforming the conventional multifamily housing typology in New York. Its distinct corner location, straddling two zoning districts, heavily influences the building's structure and layout. Along Vanderbilt, it aligns with a row of townhouses, rising to four stories. On Myrtle Avenue in the Fort Greene neighborhood of Brooklyn, known for its commercial activity, the building expands to accommodate six residential floors above two commercial levels. The project explores the coalescence of these two urban forms, creating a structure that acts as a porous barrier, its tranquil inner haven contrasting with the vibrant street life outside.

The building is filled with greenery. Its staggered design offers a variety of communal outdoor spaces, each distinct in size and function. A secluded backyard extends the local streetscape; a central courtyard is enlivened by surrounding movement; and a raised public square provides. long views at a higher elevation. Abundant shared external spaces encourage residents to enjoy outdoor living, neighborly interactions, and engagement with the building as a community within a community.

Isometric

Site Plan, 1:1,000

Section, 1:500

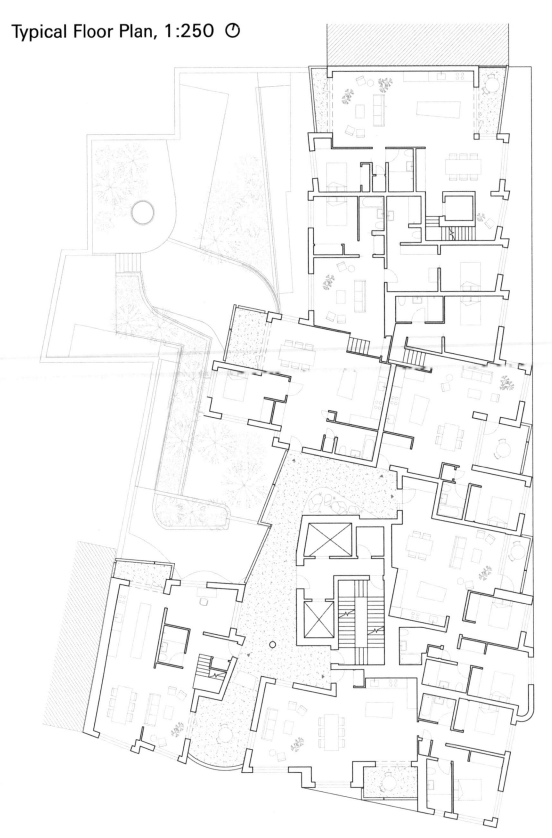

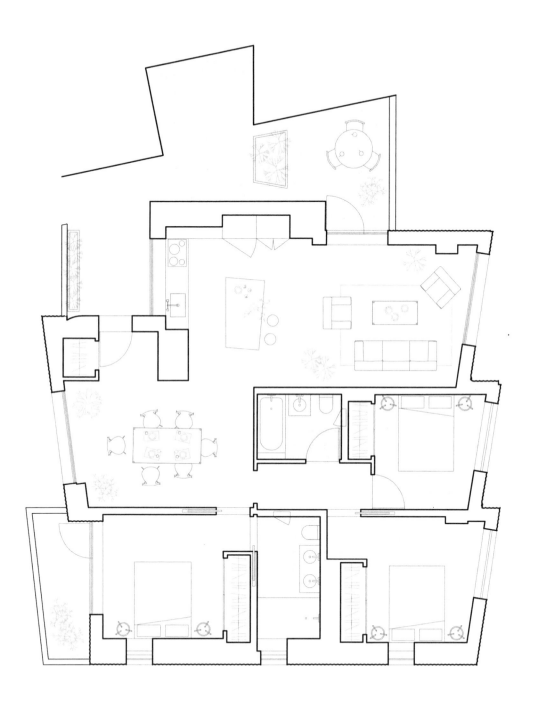

Study Model

Physical Model

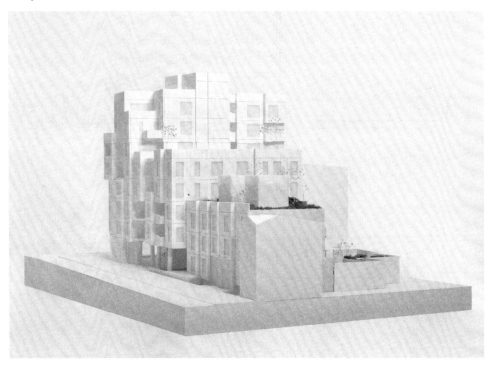

Physical Model

450 UNION
BROOKLYN, NEW YORK, USA

Located in the Gowanus area of Brooklyn, 450 Union is an ambitious exploration of porosity, connectivity, community, and affordability in urban living. This project continues our investigation of the potential of nonstandard circulation, terraces, and zoning setbacks to create outdoor living spaces that enrich the dense urban fabric.

The site encompasses approximately 2,650 square meters at the intersection of Union Street and Bond Street, extending to the Gowanus Canal waterfront. Units are designed to maximize views and engagement with the surroundings. Lower units enjoy a close connection with the Gowanus Canal and the nearby Carroll Gardens neighborhood, while the upper floors provide views of the Manhattan and Brooklyn skylines. The building's rotational alignment with the canal ensures long views for each unit, either toward the city's downtown or along the canal, while allowing for secondary orientation and multiple points of access to daylight.

The building's massing encloses a verdant courtyard, extending the public waterfront park into the residents' private domain. Terraces link to commercial levels on Union and Bond streets, creating cascading gardens that enhance the urban green space. The building's character is further shaped by its material selection, with gray iron-spot brick and blue-green mortar creating an uncommon yet harmonious aesthetic. These explorations into materiality, massing, and unit layout work together to offer a fresh take on urban living in a neighborhood quickly redefining its identity.

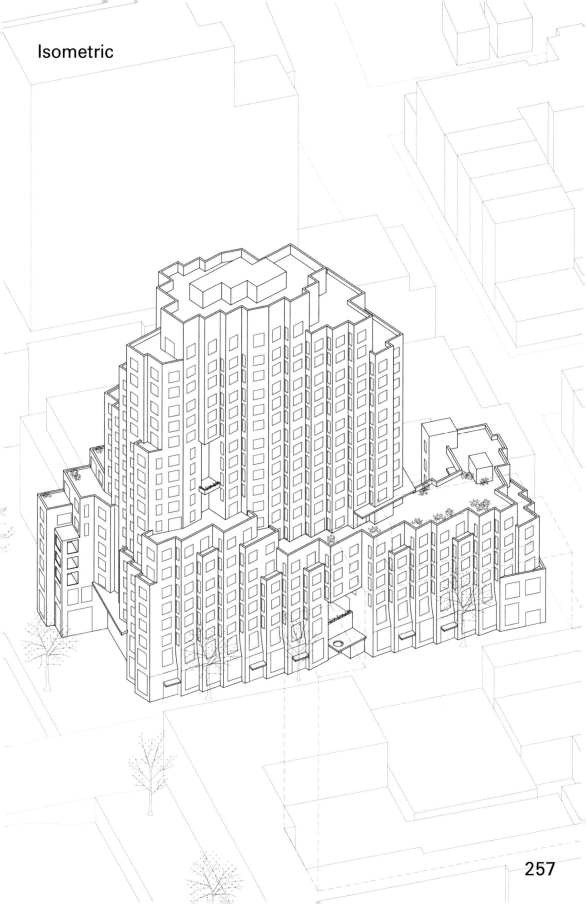

Site Plan, 1:1,000 ○

Section, 1:500

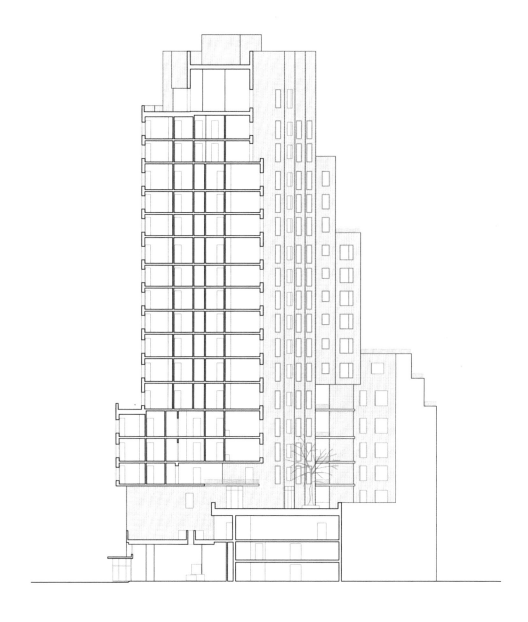

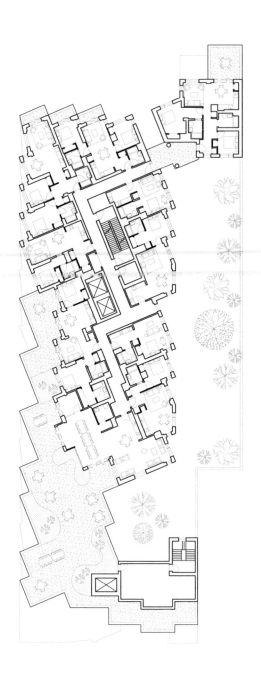

Unit Plan, 1:100

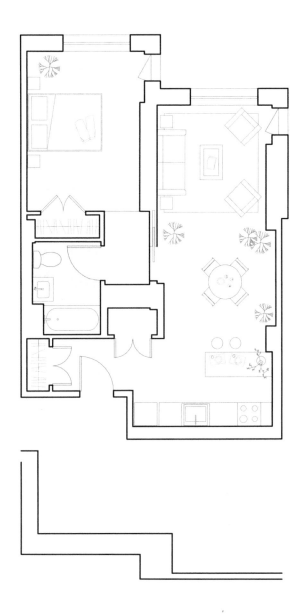

Physical Model

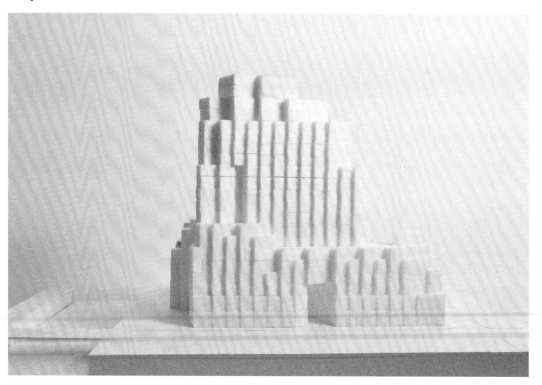

Physical Model

Physical Model

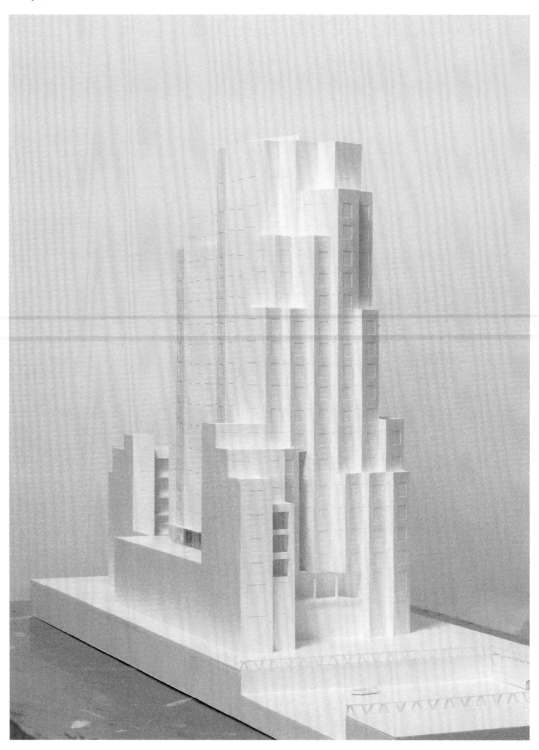

Las Americas aims to curb environmentally and socially
density low-income housing for migrant workers from

266

unsustainable urban sprawl, acting as a prototype for higher-
surrounding rural areas

Working with the city of León, a site was chosen close to public

transport, hospitals, schools, and playgrounds

An existing market, important for the local economy, became

A newly renovated playground adjoins the building

Entry into the building is located just off its tallest corner,
anchoring the neighborhood with a civic gesture

Las Américas just before move-in

The busy market snuggles up close to the building

Soft, brutalist architecture provides a backdrop for vibrant,

The day before move-in

with low-maintenance native plants

A journey home along shared outdoor corridors

Passing neighbors on the way home from work

A moment of tranquility after sunset

The nearby playground stays active into the night

PROJECT DATA

BREATHE

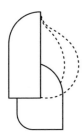

GFA	60 sqm
Stories	4
Location	Milan, Italy
Status	Built 2017

BERGEN

GFA	330 sqm
Lot Area	190 sqm
Stories	4
Location	Brooklyn, NY, USA
Status	Built 2020

CLIFTON

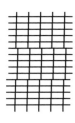

GFA	420 sqm
Lot Area	210 sqm
Stories	3
Location	Brooklyn, NY, USA
Status	Built 2021

Client	MINI Living
Team	Florian Idenburg, Jing Liu, Ilias Papageorgiou, Ian Ollivier, Pietro Pagliaro, Isabel Sarasa, Iason Houssein, Álvaro Gómez-Sellés
Collaborators	Xilografia Nuova Srl
Structure	Light-gauge steel
Facade	TiO_2-Coated Mesh Membrane

Client	Elizabeth Beer, Brian Janusiak
Team	Jing Liu, Álvaro Gómez-Sellés, Andrew Fu, Sanger Clark, Yuanjun Summer Liu, Ray Rui Wu
Structure	Concrete masonry unit, steel
Facade	Brick

Client	Janaina Tschäpe
Team	Jing Liu, Sophie Nichols, Andrew Gibbs, Emma Silverblatt
Structure	Concrete masonry unit, wood
Facade	Concrete masonry unit

9 CHAPEL

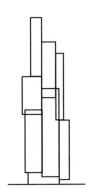

GFA	5,180 sqm
Lot Area	460 sqm
Residential	3,850 sqm
Shared	670 sqm
Units	27
Stories	14
Location	Brooklyn, NY, USA
Status	Built 2024

PARTY WALL

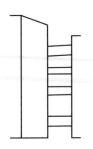

GFA	770 sqm
Lot Area	310 sqm
Residential	430 sqm
Shared	270 sqm
Units	16
Stories	5
Location	Athens, Greece
Status	Competition 2010

PETALHOUSE

GFA	60 sqm
Stories	1
Location	Los Angeles, CA, USA
	Prototype Accessory Dwelling Unit
Status	Competition 2020

Client	Tankhouse
Team	Florian Idenburg, Ted Baab, Karilyn Johanesen, Martina Baratta, Andrew Gibbs, Deok Kyu Chung, Ray Rui Wu
Collaborators	Architect of Record: Kane AUD; Structure: Silman; MEP: Consulting Engineering Services; Envelope: Laufs Engineering Design; Lighting Designer: Lighting Workshop; Expediter: William Vitacco Associates
Structure	In-situ concrete
Facade	Metal rainscreen, concrete masonry unit

Client	Oliaros SA
Team	Florian Idenburg, Jing Liu, Ilias Papageorgiou, Iannis Kandyliaris, Cheong Kang Park
Structure	In-situ concrete
Facade	Wall and window system

Client	City of Los Angeles, CA
Team	Florian Idenburg, Ted Baab, Yuanjun Summer Liu
Collaborators	Structure: John A. Martin Associates, Inc.
Structure	Cross-laminated timber
Facade	Metal rainscreen

ADELPHI

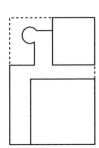

GFA	760 sqm
Lot Area	420 sqm
Units	House + Office
Stories	2
Location	Brooklyn, NY, USA
Status	Expected completion 2025

450 WARREN

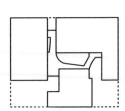

GFA	5,020 sqm
Lot Area	1,160 sqm
Residential	3,250 sqm
Shared	840 sqm
Commercial	410 sqm
Units	18
Parking	9
Stories	5
Location	Brooklyn, NY, USA
Status	Built 2022

TINY

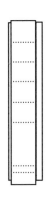

GFA	3,500 sqm
Lot Area	440 sqm
Residential	2,230 sqm
Shared	1,070 sqm
Commercial	200 sqm
Units	96
Stories	17
Location	New York, NY, USA
Status	Competition 2012

Client	Florian Idenburg, Jing Liu
Team	Jing Liu, Florian Idenburg, Emma Silverblatt, Ray Rui Wu, Sean Broadhurst
Collaborators	Structure: Silman; MEP: LL Engineering; Lighting: O-N-P; Geotechnical Engineer: GZA, SET; Expediter: William Vitacco Associates
Structure	Steel
Facade	Concrete canvas, metal rainscreen

Client	Tankhouse
Team	Florian Idenburg, Jing Liu, Ted Baab, Karilyn Johanesen, Deok Kyu Chung, Alek Tomich, Danny Wei
Collaborators	Architect of Record: Kane AUD; Structure: Silman; MEP: ABS Engineering; Envelope: Laufs Engineering Design; Lighting Designer: Lighting Workshop; Expediter: William Vitacco Associates; Landscape: Brooklyn Grange, Gowanus Canal Conservancy
Structure	In-situ concrete
Facade	Concrete masonry unit

Client	New York Department of Housing Preservation and Development
Team	Florian Idenburg, Jing Liu, Ilias Papageorgiou, Ted Baab, Thilde Bjørkskov, Alicia Hergenroeder, Richard Duff, Ivan Kostic
Collaborators	Development: Alloy; Affordable Housing Partner: Camba; Structure: Guy Nordenson Associates; MEP/Energy: Right Environment
Structure	Pre-cast concrete
Facade	Pre-cast concrete panel

LAS AMÉRICAS

GFA	6,040 sqm
Lot Area	2,010 sqm
Residential	3,530 sqm
Shared	1,620 sqm
Commercial	130 sqm
Units	56
Parking	25
Stories	6
Location	León, Mexico
Status	Built 2021

144 VANDERBILT

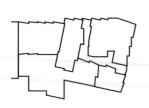

GFA	7,510 sqm
Lot Area	1,640 sqm
Residential	3,860 sqm
Shared	2,140 sqm
Commercial	750 sqm
Units	26
Parking	18
Stories	9
Location	Brooklyn, NY, USA
Status	Expected completion 2024

450 UNION

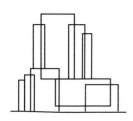

GFA	20,360 sqm
Lot Area	2,650 sqm
Residential	11,200 sqm
Shared	5,840 sqm
Commercial	2,110 sqm
Units	158
Parking	24
Stories	20
Location	Brooklyn, NY, USA
Status	Expected completion 2026

Client	IMUVI Development City of León
Team	Florian Idenburg, Jing Liu, Ilias Papageorgiou, Ted Baab, Isabel Sarasa, Seunghyun Kang, Sophie Nichols, Pam Anantrungroj
Collaborators	IMUVI León, ICNUM, CIE, COSEBA
Structure	In-situ concrete
Facade	Concrete masonry unit

Client	Tankhouse
Team	Florian Idenburg, Jing Liu, Ted Baab, Jonathan Molloy, Melissa Gutiérrez Soto, Dohyun Lee, Deok Kyu Chung
Collaborators	Architect of Record: Kane AUD; Structure: Silman; MEP: ABS Engineering; Envelope: Entuitive; Lighting: Office of Natalia Priwin; Expediter: William Vitacco Associates; Landscape: Watson Salembier
Structure	In-situ concrete
Facade	Pre-cast concrete panel, brick

Client	Tankhouse, MacArthur Holdings
Team	Florian Idenburg, Jing Liu, Karilyn Johanesen, Amin Tadj, Emma Silverblatt, Fabian Puller, Demetri Lampris, Madeline Kim, Sean Broadhurst, Yuanjun Summer Liu, Tracy Tan, Risako Arcari, Pa Ramyarupa
Collaborators	Architect of Record: Magnusson Architecture and Planning; Structure: Thornton Tomasetti; MEP: Derive Engineers; Envelope: Laufs Engineering Design; Expediter: William Vitacco Associates; Lighting: Map Design Studio; Landscape: Michael Van Valkenburgh Associates, Inc.
Structure	In-situ concrete
Facade	Brick

CODA
FLORIAN IDENBURG

In the thicket of contemporary demands, we find ourselves adrift, increasingly removed from the essence of our art. The simple act of creating shelter – architecture's foundational myth – has been overshadowed by the mercantile, transforming our profession into selling lifestyle commodities while struggling to meet increasingly unattainable targets. Architects are at the mercy of those who control resources: land, materials, energy, labor, and capital. Yet it's the architect's role to transform these resources into the spaces we can call home.

The entirety of the world's population requires some form of shelter. Beyond the quarter that lives informally and the very few who can afford a custom home, most dwellings are designed for a universal and generic figure: a student, a young family, a retiree, etc. Current economic mechanisms reduce residents to consumers, ordered into neat categories and identities. Yet each individual life possesses a richness and complexity that defy such simple classification. How much more intricate is the variety of settings when it includes families, groups, partnerships, friends, or any conceivable human constellation? Designing multifamily housing compels us to balance the spectrum of human needs – from the broadly functional to the deeply personal. When creating a home for unknown inhabitants, how can we give it character, and how can this be done in a conglomerate, collective, and affordable order?

Beyond affordable specificity, collective housing requires much more. We live in a world increasingly obsessed with fear. One's home is the last "safe space." From this vantage point, we observe the exterior with ever more angst. While technology has ostensibly brought the outside world in, our devices have siloed us. The public realm has become fragmented, contained, compressed, and trapped behind ever-thinner layers of glass. As the noise levels within our online echo chambers have swelled to insufferable levels, we swipe the world away and go about our day, desensitized. How do we craft buildings that offer comfort yet allow people to remain connected to society and civic life, even during uncertain times? Can our homes defend our humanity by providing space for sociality, contemplation, and connection with our actual neighbors, real-life communities, and our direct environment? The diversity of in-person communities allows us exposure to "that which is other." How can a building foster these bonds?

Housing is driven by numbers. The pressures of market-driven urbanization have purged most ideals out of our homes. Housing became the building blocks of urban life and, along with it, private life. Historically, buildings adorned with outgrowths, from ornament and colonnades to bay windows and verandas, created space "in between" – a deepened zone for life in the crevices. These areas foster particularity and connection, and offer shelter for various life-forms. In our current data-obsessed world, dimensions and measurements are all-encompassing. Depth is a liability in a drive for optimization. The thinner a facade, the more efficient a building. The flatter and less articulated, the better the pro forma. Yet this approach squeezes out the ambiguous zones between inside and outside, between home and city, between protected and exposed. In our effort to flatten everything, life is purged out.

The designs in this book, often inadvertently defiant, breathe through their porousness. Diverse in their approach, these projects share a common resistance to the formulaic – each a unique exploration of the potential of space. We peel away the layers between the urban and the personal, delving into deep zones where serendipitous encounters are framed, not merely transpire. Beyond mere entries and corridors, our exploration extends to spaces that introduce a layer of civic-ness within the interior world. Balconies and windows are more than openings; they are portals to a world where boundaries are softened, where the home extends its embrace to the street.

Within these fluid borders, an assortment of life-forms – plants, animals, and human connections – create a tapestry rich with potential.

With this book, we attempt to capture something intangible in words and images. With sincere optimism, we seek to knit small pockets of freedom within the complexity of urban housing today. If *Order, Edge, Aura* was our birth cry, this book is a plea for a return to consciousness in how we conceive homes for the masses. Let us rethink our approach to architecture and recognize the profound layers and connections that make a space truly a home.

BIOGRAPHIES

Ted Baab runs his own practice, BAAB, in Brooklyn focused on both houses and housing. He teaches at the Cooper Union, where he works on housing design, and coordinates first-year design studios around techniques of architectural geometry. He worked at SO–IL for eleven years, leading many of the firm's housing projects.

Florian Idenburg is co-founder of SO–IL and Professor of the Practice at Cornell University. His grandmother's house was designed by her uncle H. P. Berlage. On her veranda, he learned firsthand the benefits of the space in between.

Karilyn Johanesen is a senior associate at SO–IL and visiting lecturer at Cornell University. She has been involved in the design and implementation of all of SO–IL's projects with Brooklyn developer Tankhouse, equipping her with advanced experience in the intricacies of residential projects.

Nicolas Kemper is the publisher of the *New York Review of Architecture*. Trained as an architect, he also teaches at the School of Visual Arts and the Kean School of Public Architecture, and volunteers as a tour guide at the Cathedral of Saint John the Divine. He hopes one day to live in a home with a front porch.

Jing Liu, born in 1980 in China, is a founding partner at SO–IL. She grew up on three continents and in five cities, losing all of her childhood homes to neoliberal development. She currently teaches at universities on the East Coast of the United States and works from her base in Brooklyn, New York.

Iwan Baan (b. 1975) is a Dutch architecture and documentary photographer based in Amsterdam. His photographs document the life of architecture around the world, from informal and traditional housing structures to the growth of megacities, and how individuals, communities, and societies reappropriate their built environment to make it their own. Baan has worked with leading architects and architecture studios. His images are regularly published in newspapers and magazines. His work is exhibited internationally.

Naho Kubota (born in Iida, Japan) is an artist and photographer based in New York.

IMAGE CREDITS

With the exception of those listed on page 319, images are
© SO–IL

We have made every effort to identify all relevant rights hold-
ers. In those instances where we have not been able to locate
and / or notify the rights holder(s), we ask that they contact
the publisher.

144 VANDERBILT
IWAN BAAN

Tagged neighboring wall

329

Brooklyn around the corner

Downtown Brooklyn at arm's length

"Bricking" it

UNDER CONSTRUCTION
IWAN BAAN, FLORIAN IDENBURG, DEAN KAUFMAN,
FIELD CONDITION

Hoisting light-gauge steel structures of Breathe with mobile crane

Hoisting by hands

Hoisting by pulley

Amazing climber

Amazing sewing

9 Chapel's porous envelope against the neighbors

Light layers

Catching up with football

Stair and water tower

Framing the sky

Facade mock-up

Installing the mesh

Skeleton of 144 Vanderbilt

Shifting terrace slabs

Community spaces below street level

Installing pre-cast facade panels

Skeleton of Las Américas

Custom concrete blocks

Framing the courtyard

Installing the blocks

Bergen facade

Bricking it

Proud bricklayer at Bergen

Clifton facade mock-up

Facade

Punch-listing

450 Union mortar

450 Union facade

Demolition continues at 450 Union

Ridding the site of spirits at Adelphi groundbreaking

Discovering an Ice Age boulder

Lunch time at Adelphi

Concrete canvas facade